How an Engineering Professor
Becomes a Spiritual Philosopher

Diary of a 21st Century Human Soul

Dr. Tommy S. W. Wong

Dedicated to

my parents, Wong Sze Fong and Woo En Yueh

my parents-in-law, Sum Chip Shing and Ko Luk Ying

my darling wife, Christina

and my wonderful sons, Alston, Lester and Hanson

Acknowledgement

I like to thank the Great Spirit for selecting me as an instrument in authoring this book for the benefit of mankind.

Preface

Have you met an engineering professor? Have you met an engineering professor who is deep into spirituality and writes spiritual books? I have, and he is me.

I had worked as an engineering professor in a university in Singapore. I now write philosophical, self-help and spiritual books. For an engineering professor to become a spiritual author is unusual to say the least. Indeed, it is this unusualness that prompted me to write this book. Engineering and spirituality are often perceived as two ends of a spectrum, and it is. As engineering deals with the physical, and spirituality deals with the non-physical, there is actually tremendous synergy once they are combined. In this book, there are ten chapters in which I share my physical and spiritual journey. They are: (1) Study years, (2) Working years, (3) Academic years, (4) From an engineering professor to a spiritual author, (5) Care for the dying, (6) Being unemployed, (7) Return as consultant, (8) Into politics and socio-political writings, (9) Becoming a spiritual philosopher, and (10) Epilogue.

You are invited to join me on this journey. I hope this sharing is beneficial to you. May your life be filled with peace, love, joy and harmony!

Tommy S. W. Wong
Singapore
July 2016

Table of Contents

Chapter 1

Study years

I was born in Hong Kong on 14 December 1952. Between 1956-60, I attended my kindergarten and the first year of primary school at St. Mary's Church College, Hong Kong. Thereafter, I joined St. Paul's College, Hong Kong to continue my primary school education and also the first two years' of my secondary school education (1960-67). At St. Paul's College, we used to receive a report sheet on a quarterly basis. On the sheets, test or examination grades were shown, which were meant to reflect our academic performance. A pass grade was shown in blue color, and a fail grade was shown in red. Every time I received my report sheet, there were some red grades among the blue grades. Clearly, I was not a good student as for even average students; their report sheets would be all blue. But then I thought my report sheets were "better", because they were more colorful. And then during the teacher-parent sessions, which my mother would attend, the teachers would be very kind to tell her that I was an above-average student. My mother would then leave the school "happily". In truth, I was of course a below-average student – but see what happened to my studies, later.

In 1967, I moved to England and continued my secondary school education at Mayfield College. With the change of environment, I made a significant improvement in my study. In 1969, I completed my Ordinary Level (O-level) examinations and left Mayfield College with a respectable five O-level passes in British History, Chemistry, Chinese, Foreign History, and Mathematics. I then joined Woolwich College in London, which supposedly had a better teaching system supported by better teachers as compared to Mayfield, and they did have. At Woolwich, I pursued my Advanced Level (A-level) studies.

Apart from changing college and location, in terms of living style, there was also a major shift. Mayfield was a boarding school in which they took care of the meals, laundry of the boarders. The students supposedly only had to be concerned with their studies. However, the life in the boarding school was very much regimented. We had to follow a rigid routine of study, play, eat, rest and so on. On the other hand, when I moved to Woolwich, I rented an apartment outside the college and stayed on my own. For the first time in my life, I had to do my own marketing, cooking, washing, laundry and cleaning of the apartment (i.e. daily living). Also, I had to take care of my finances, transportation, repairs in the apartment and any personal illnesses. Only after all these, did I take care my studies. I also had to discipline myself so that there was a balance between study and leisure. Although there were a lot to manage and all on my own, I loved it. The best part was freedom. I felt that I had control of my life and my destiny – an important life lesson. I was also more than happy to take responsibility for any outcome. As it happened, with the "perfect" environment at Woolwich, I excelled in my studies. In 1971, when I left Woolwich College, I scored grade A in three A-level subjects (Applied Mathematics, Physics, and Pure Mathematics), in addition to a grade B in an A-level endorsement (Electronics) and a Grade E in Classical Chinese. These results are of course a far cry from those I received at St. Paul's College where they were mixtures of red and blue grades. How often do we just use a single criterion to determine whether a period is successful or otherwise? For students, it is often the examination results. Hence, using this criterion, my time at Woolwich was successful. But actually there were other "major" successes. Personally, I consider my total management of study, marketing, cooking, washing, laundry and cleaning the apartment was a major success. Indeed, this is one of the great benefits when students leave home to live and study on their own. In such a situation, students do not only gain academic knowledge but also skills on independent living – a real-life learning.

Another major success was meeting an extremely good and kind man, Gurchetan Saggu, who was my classmate and a good friend for decades. On one occasion in the early 1970s, I had to drive from London to Leeds in north England. Since I was not too familiar with the roads in London, Gurchetan agreed to accompany me until I found road signs which would lead me to the motorway going to Leeds. After driving for awhile, I already found the road sign and should have dropped Gurchetan off so that he could go home. But for my self-interest of having a companion, I continued driving north. Eventually, we ended up at a remote part of London and far away from Gurchetan's home, then I dropped him off. From that remote part of London, it was difficult for Gurchetan to find transport to go home. He didn't complain. Instead, he wished me a pleasant journey ahead.

On another occasion in the late 1990s, Gurchetan had been suffering from a persistent illness for some time. His doctor advised him that he may get better by taking a holiday. He decided to come all the way to Singapore with his family and have an expensive holiday with me. Under the circumstances, I ought to be a good host. Unfortunately, due to the pressure and frustrations

4

at work, I treated Gurchetan and his family poorly, but he never complained. On the day when they flew back to London, I only dropped them at the airport and didn't even see them off. That was the last time I saw Gurchetan. He passed away in 2007.

With my excellent A-level results, I entered the university and the course of my first choice.

Before I describe my university days, let us take a detour. Apart from receiving secular education, I also received religious education in those early years. St. Paul's College was a Christian school, and Mayfield College was a Catholic school. Despite these early influences, religion had little or no impact on me. Even during my adulthood when I read many more books and attended many more talks of different faiths, I still did not find the teachings or people within those groups appealing enough for me to join them. In fact, in those days, I would attend one talk and seldom return to the same group because I found the talk so unappealing. I was really an atheist at that time and used to ridicule people of faiths. Subsequently, as I moved through religions into non-religious spirituality, I found a type of spirituality that appealed to my inner-self. Then, I understood why I didn't find those religious teachings appealing. Nowadays, I like to think I am very spiritual and non-religious. Indeed, you could say that I belong to the "spiritual but not religious" group. But then, there is no physical group that I belong to. Personalities like Shirley MacLaine and Oprah Winfrey also practice this type of spirituality. Spiritually speaking, I can see how the Great Spirit has been active in my life – before and after I became spiritual.

When students come to choose a university to further their studies, they will usually choose one that is academically strong in the course that they intend to study. But for me, I used a completely unorthodox criterion when I chose mine. I wanted to study at a university where there was an excellent professional football team near that university. In this way, I figured that I could watch excellent football while receiving my university education. At that time, Leeds United was the best or one of the best football teams in England. Based on my unorthodox criterion, I chose Leeds University. As for the course, I chose civil engineering because I thought it was a good way to make the world better. Later in life, I found another way outside engineering which can be more powerful in changing the world.

On the footballing side, I was richly rewarded. On 16 October 1971, I watched the "great" Leeds United live for the first time, and they beat Manchester City 3-0. There were the legendary players like Billy Bremner (captain), Allan Clarke and Peter Lorimer. The team was superbly managed by Don Revie. Indeed, during my first year at Leeds, they won the Football Association (FA) Cup – the only time they won the Cup in their history. They also came second in the English Football League in that 1971-72 season. During my second year, they came third in the League, and runners-up in both the Union of European Football Associations (UEFA) Cup Winners' Cup and the FA Cup. During my third and final year, they became the League champions - only the second time in their history. Not only did they win the League in the 1973-74 season, they also set up a 29-match unbeaten run of league matches from the start of the season. In fact, during my three years at Leeds, it was their most successful period. You see I really made the "right" choice to study at Leeds. In 1974, I completed my course and left Leeds, this coincided with the decline of Leeds United. What I leant from the fortune of Leeds United is that to be successful, you need good management, good players, good supporting staff but above all, you need a good supporter like me, haha!

On the academic side, it was somewhat uneventful. While most university graduates would say that the university days were the best days of their lives, it wasn't for me. There were subsequent periods which I found were much more fulfilling. On the other hand, out of this uneventful period, I learned one thing. In life, if it is plain sailing, there are few challenges to help us grow as a human or a spiritual being. Anyway, I enjoyed my time at Leeds. In particular, since there were only one or two Chinese in my class, I enjoyed the company of my English classmates and friends, like Arthur Pearson and Nigel Sporne in particular. During the university vacations, I used to go and stay at their homes. So, I had first-hand experience of what loving English families were like. I am still in touch with Arthur and Nigel today in 2016. Back to my study, with my brilliant A-level results, I suppose I was expecting to graduate with a first-class honors degree. When the results came out, I was only awarded an upper second-class honors Bachelor of Science (BSc) degree. For most students, they would be more than happy with my result. However for me, it was a disappointment. So, you see how expectations shape our reactions. In any case, in addition to the degree, the university was kind enough to award me the John Illingworth Prize for a meritorious performance over the three years. I suppose it was a good consolation! I received the degree and the prize when I attended the convocation on 17 July 1974.

After graduating from Leeds University, I had the option of pursuing the Doctor of Philosophy (PhD) degree at Leeds or Cambridge University. Since the latter was more prestigious (I mean Sir Issac Newton went there), I decided to go to Cambridge. In fact, it was also the prestige and not so much the academic knowledge that made me decide to pursue the PhD degree. You know you can change your title from Mr. to Dr. after you receive your PhD degree. In addition, it was also my father's wish to have a son with a PhD. My father never had the opportunity to study at a university, so he was living his dream in his son (that's me). For all these "wrong" reasons, I struggled at Cambridge. Not only was the academic standard higher at Cambridge, but I really had no idea on how to do research. PhD is a research degree.

> Fast forward to my later years, how interesting that I was unable to acquire research skills in one of the very top universities in England. Later on, when I was working in a lower ranked university in

Singapore, I became a "good" researcher and won an international research award.

At that time and towards the end of my first year, I submitted the project report *"The Production of Perfect Harmonic Motion in Water"*. I then attended the oral examination. After the examination, the university decided that I wasn't suitable to carry on with the PhD programme and asked (read told) me to leave. But for my effort in that year, they awarded me the Certificate of Post-graduate study in Engineering.

While the entire episode appeared to be a failure, there was actually an enlightening moment. At Cambridge, while students carried out their academic study at a department, they were also affiliated to a college for their non-academic activities. I was affiliated to Trinity Hall College. At that time at the college, occasionally they would arrange an academic to give a talk followed by a discussion. The students affiliated to that college were free to attend. I attended one of these talks. While I can't recall the exact topic for discussion, I can recall it was related to morality or ethics. The speaker highlighted that if there were more than 50% supporting the issue, would it make it ethical? Would it be unethical if less than 50% supporting the issue? This occasion awakened me how cultural England was. People in this country would spend time and effort to discuss issues that were completely unrelated to making money. After I left England and returned to Asia, there was hardly any discussion of this kind. This occasion planted a seed in me that to be a cultured or human society, that society has to contemplate issues that are beyond money. How this seed blossomed in my later years!

After I was told that I had to leave Cambridge, it actually produced wonderful encounters. Rev. David Isitt who was the reverend at Trinity Hall College, somehow found out what was happening to me. Although he hardly knew me, he made the effort to contact and talked to me to see how he could help. At that time, my father was with me having a holiday in Cambridge. After David had a better understanding of the situation, he arranged a lunch meeting with my father. At the meeting, he advised my father that the most important thing to do at that time was not to make me feel like a "failure". Don't you think this is sound advice? David, indeed a wise and kind man, even kept in touch with the failure (me) for the subsequent 30+ years until his passing in 2009 as Canon Isitt. You know most people in our societies are only interested in keeping in touch with achievers. How fortunate that I met one person who was prepared to keep in touch with a failure. Apart from David, I also received other supports. Even friends who were not so close also came and rallied around me. It's indeed times like this (when I was down and out) that I found out who my true friends were. I am most grateful to all their supports!

From the Cambridge episode, I learned that it is not beneficial to both parties if we live other people's dreams in our lives or live our dreams in other people's lives. Why not let everyone just live their own dreams in their own lives? See how this has influenced me in my relationships with my sons in later years.

After being "kicked-out" of Cambridge, I really had to ponder on what to do next. Apparently I was not good at research, and better at classroom study and taking examinations. Since I was still motivated to study rather than say taking a job, I applied to Birmingham University to study water resources technology. I was prepared to study for one more year before starting to work. Even though this course was supposedly coursework based, in fact it had a large project (research) component. The proportions of coursework and project components were about 50-50. As it happened, I enjoyed the project work immensely and produced a very good project report on *"An Investigation of the Steady State Spatially Varied Flow Profiles with Increasing Discharge"*. At the end of the 12-month study, I attended the convocation on 17 December 1976 and received the Master of Science (MSc) degree. I also came third in the class, which can be considered a successful end to my full-time study.

This success tasted so much sweeter after the Cambridge episode – a real case of after the bitter comes the sweet.

Thereafter, I ventured into the big wide working world.

Chapter 2

Working years

Even when I was less than half-way through the course at Birmingham, I started to apply for jobs as I had decided upon graduation that I would go out to work and not pursue anymore further study. Among several job applications, I secured one job offer from Wessex Water Authority on 29 May 1976. This was very good because it was well before my graduation. I was attracted to work for a water authority because of the very pleasant experience I had when I worked for the Medway Water Board at Chatham, England in the summer 1972. I was working as a student trainee after completing my first year of the course at Leeds University. In fact, it was so good that I returned to Medway during the following Christmas break. Back to the offer from Wessex, at that time, while it was easy for my English counterparts to get jobs, it was not easy for a Chinese like me. Hence, in a way, I was fortunate to receive the offer. After due considerations, I accepted it on 8 June 1976.

So, my first job was with Wessex and I was based at Bath – one of the most beautiful cities in England. In hindsight, I can see that I have been blessed with living and working in beautiful places on more than one occasion. I started my working life on 1 November 1976. I joined the Planning Department and was fortunate to work under the team leader Dennis Grimshaw - a competent engineer who guided me through my initial working days. In fact, even during my subsequent years at Wessex, I found the engineers were very professional in their work. Indeed, I would say I acquired professionalism from them. My first project was *"Computer rainfall-runoff modeling of the River Bristol Frome catchment"*. Interestingly, about 40 years later, my "last" engineering project was also on computer rainfall-runoff modeling. So, some things can last for an entire working life! I was so happy at that time, much more than the university days. One main reason was that I felt I was making a useful contribution to society. Of course, I did not and could not have this feeling while studying. At Wessex, I was also one of the rare Chinese among my colleagues – a situation that made me feel an achiever. So, I was very happy working at Wessex. In fact, I was thinking how come they were paying me to enjoy myself. Of course getting paid for what we do brings another great satisfaction. So, it is possible to do work that we love and also get paid for it. By the way, later on in life, I have also experienced doing the work that I loved but got very little pay for it. So, it is not true that if we work on our passion, we would automatically be rewarded financially! The happy days at Wessex were such a contrast to the unhappy days at Cambridge. This shows that it may not be a good idea to choose what we do based on prestige.

On another note, during my first year at Bath, I stayed at a hostel run by the Young Men's Christian Association (YMCA). Thereafter, as it appeared to be a long-term stay (I was actually prepared to settle down there), my father supported me to buy a four-bedroom town house. The idea was that the house was an investment as well as a holiday home for my parents and family. So, all my independent living skills that I acquired at Woolwich were well used here. However, I needed more skills such as buying and maintaining the house, furniture and electrical appliances. Fortunately, I had very helpful colleagues and there were many of them, such as Tony Bray and Adrian Walker, who would readily help me in terms of time, effort and expertise. I was really impressed by their helpfulness and extremely appreciative of their effort as I could hardly offer anything in return. This gave me first-hand experience of people in this world who would help for nothing or practically nothing. Largely due to this experience, later in life, I did likewise. This also shows that it is better to teach by action rather than words. Now back to the house, it was obvious that the house was under-utilized when my family was not having holidays in Bath. Through contacts, I rented one or more rooms out to colleague and students. So, I also gained the experience of being a landlord. Interestingly, several decades later, I became a "real" landlord.

The main things I enjoyed at that time were my independence and freedom. It was a complete carefree life with no major worries. What a difference from this care-free living to my later years when I had to live with the responsibility of looking after my extended family of three generations.

In terms of engineering work, after my first computer modeling project, I joined the Design Department and carried out designs of several river improvement schemes, which included spillways and stilling basins. I then moved out to site and supervised the construction of the extension to the Melksham Sewage Treatment Works. When I returned from site, I was meant to settle down in my "permanent" position in the Planning Department. So, over that period, I was involved in the projects *"Development of water supply strategy for Bristol Avon Division"*, *"Feasibility study of Potterne balancing reservoir"*, and *"Investigation on the upgrading of Chitterne water supply system"*. All in all, the experiences were interesting and varied.

In England, to pursue a career in civil engineering, it is important to gain the professional qualification "Chartered Engineer". To expedite the process, it is possible to sign up to a formal 3-year training programme. The disbenefit of signing up is that one is then committed to an organization for three years. On the other hand, the benefit is that the experience gained on the programme should be relevant to the subsequent professional examination. As I was keen to gain the qualification in a shortest possible time, I signed up for the programme with Wessex. While I diligently did my work for more than three years, when I completed my programme and took my professional examination, the result shows that I failed miserably. It was so bad that I was "asked" to repeat everything. Basically, I was required to gain the "right" experience by working for another three years before I could take the examination again - but I was on the formal programme. This of course was a major blow to my engineering career. Spiritually speaking, how could this happen to a decent human being who was committed to engineering? Interestingly, I had another similar experience later in life. So, why do they teach the "untruth" that *"When you do good, good things will happen to you"*? As it turned out, with the benefit of all these experiences, I gained a much deeper spiritual insight.

In terms of the examination result, my time at Wessex was a disaster. Fortunately, I had sympathetic colleagues who rallied around me and supported me emotionally. Actually, apart from the examinations result, I had a wonderful time at Wessex - a time that I treasure even today in 2016. This shows that there is more to life than examination results.

During my first working year at Wessex, my brother Commy was pursuing his second year PhD programme at Edinburgh University in Scotland. Unfortunately, maybe due to the stress of his studies, he was diagnosed with an affective disorder, and suffered his first mental breakdown in February 1977. While he at first still tried to stay on the programme, it was apparent later that his illness was too serious. So, he terminated his studies and took a rest. Thereafter, he found a job with Essex Health Authority and then with Computer Analysts and Programmers (CAP) in London. While he was working, he suffered a relapse and a second mental breakdown occurred in 1979. In fact, at times, his condition was so bad that he had to be hospitalized for an extended period. On reflection, this incident showed how good the medical system in England was. My brother's hospitalization, including consultation and medication, was completely free because in England, they have the National Health Service (NHS). This indeed shows that England is not just a cultured society, but also a humane society. Without the NHS, can you imagine the financial burden my family would have had to carry? This of course would be on top of our emotional and psychological concerns for Commy's health and future. Finally, upon physicians' advice, since Commy's condition was long-term and incurable, it was considered best for him to return home so that he would have the full support of the family. Commy left England for Hong Kong in 1979. In view of Commy's condition and other family issues, I was also planning to return to Hong Kong.

After Commy's departure, I stayed on to take the professional examination. After the release of my examination result, it was a clear that I should move on. I therefore resigned and left Wessex on 2 September 1980. Soon after, I also left England after having lived and being immersed in its culture for 13 years. I am glad to say that I have acquired many of the "better" qualities of English culture.

When I returned to Hong Kong, I was completely disillusioned with engineering. I knew of others who were much less dedicated to engineering than I was, and yet they sailed through the examination. Feeling unjust and badly treated by the engineering profession, I decided to quit engineering. At that time, the Hong Kong stock market was booming. To ride on the boom, my father opened an investment company and the business was to carry out trading on the stock market only. Since there were vacancies in the company, I saw it as an opportunity to switch out of engineering. Also, it saved me the trouble of looking for a job. So, without any formal application, I joined Tung Sun Investment Company as a manager. In practice, I was working more like a stock broker or a remisier. I was not exactly the type who liked to work in a family business and as a remisier. After several months, I was already looking for a "proper" job. However, since the company was really short-handed due to the booming market, I agreed to help out for one full year. Hence, I worked for Tung Sun Investment Company from 1 October 1980 to 30 September 1981.

While switching from an engineer to a stock broker and moving from England to Hong Kong appeared to be a purely physical and an unplanned event, it was actually a plan by the Great Spirit. The string of events that prompted the switch were my brother's illness, my miserable examination results, a booming stock market and the opening of an investment company by my father. After joining the stock broking business, I was interested in learning how to profit from the stock market. At the time, there was a private school which conducted short courses on stock investment. I attended a few and they were quite good. At one of these courses, I noticed a young lady. We didn't connect then. At this school, apart from the short courses, they also organized monthly gatherings to discuss issues related to the stock market. I joined these gatherings regularly and noticed the young lady was there too. At the gathering on 5 September 1981, we had an opportunity to converse and I found out her name was Christina. We then communicated over the telephone, and went on our first date on 8 November 1981. She was very mature and understanding. Right from the start, we were so compatible that physically, we were like hand in glove, and spiritually like soulmates. After the first date, we practically went out everyday. Soon, we fell in love. I proposed to her on 13 January 1982 – a little over three months from the first date. Wouldn't you say romance was in the air? And then in just over nine months from the first date, we got married on 24 July 1982. Wouldn't you say this was a great plan by the Great Spirit? Without any of the earlier events (my brother's illness, my miserable examination result, a booming stock market, the opening of an investment company by my father, and change of career), could I have ended up marrying my soulmate Christina? Wouldn't you say while some of the events looked disastrous, in fact I was blessed in more ways than one? Also, wouldn't you also say the fees I paid for the short courses were excellent investments? I mean see the return I got. Interestingly, later in life. I have other experiences which looked similarly disastrous, yet they were really blessings in disguise.

In Hong Kong at that time, not only the stock market was booming, the civil engineering industry was also booming. They were designing and building the underground railway system, known as the Mass Transit Railway (MTR). After several months away from engineering and knowing that the financial industry was not suitable for me, I was ready to re-enter the engineering profession. With the booming market, it was not difficult for me to find a job. On 10 June 1981, I received a job offer from Charles Haswell & Partners (Far East). On 15 August 1981, I accepted the offer.

After completing my full year at Tung Sun, I immediately started work at Haswell. They were an English consultant. So, I was more comfortable with their English style of management, more like Wessex in England. From 1 October 1981 to 9 October 1983, I was a member of the team responsible for the *"Design of Sai Wan Ho station and running tunnels and ventilation shafts of Mass Transit Railway Corporation's (MTRC) Island Line project"*. During this period, I felt more settled after the change in living environment, change in culture and the flip-flop in profession. More significantly, this was the time when I started dating Christina. As it turned out, the change in profession was also significant. Subsequently, Christina confided to me that if I were a stock broker when we met, she probably wouldn't have gone out with me because she didn't like stock brokers. So, everything was for the better. After we decided to get married, we bought our own apartment in Wan Chai on Hong Kong Island and lived happily ever after! Wouldn't you say this is a fairytale come true? Do you see the divine plan?

After getting married, I was more serious with my career. In Hong Kong, there was a local professional examination for civil engineers. I successfully passed the examination and became a member of the Hong Kong Institution of Engineers on 5 August 1983. At that time, the design for the MTRC Island Line was coming to an end. Haswell was transferring their staff to other projects or laying them off. As I was a qualified engineer in Hong Kong, I could take on positions with more responsibilities. On 10 October 1983, Haswell appointed me as the resident engineer to the "*Site supervision of Hong Kong Housing Authority's Squatter Area Improvements project*". This job was challenging for me as I was used to working with professionals. On this project, I had a difficult contractor. My job was to ensure that what they built was according to the specifications. With the contractor I had, it was not an easy task. In fact, they even turned nasty later on. As innocent or ignorant as I was, I thought Haswell would back me up. Instead, they terminated my contract – a real eye opener to the real world! Fortunately, I was married then. Christina together with other friends and colleagues gave me their utmost emotional and moral supports, for which I am grateful. The contract ended on 28 February 1985. So, I was on the project for only about 17 months, and yet it felt like years. I suppose I must be relieved to leave such a "hostile" working environment. You see the Great Spirit would take us out of an undesirable situation, even though we may try hard to stay in it. Indeed, being fired by Haswell proved to be another major blessing!

Soon after getting the notification from Haswell, I naturally started looking for other jobs. At that time, the civil engineering market in Hong Kong wasn't that rosy. One reason was the near completion of the MTRC Island Line which meant that many other civil engineers were retrenched and therefore also looking for jobs. In fact, this is a common problem when a major civil engineering project ends. In view of the situation, I was looking for local as well as overseas jobs. For overseas jobs, obviously I couldn't rely on the local newspapers. So, I subscribed to England's Institution of Civil Engineers' (ICE) weekly job advertisement newsletter. This was an unusual move but subsequently proved to be most fruitful. In any case, despite the poor job market in Hong Kong, I managed to secure a job with China Overseas

Building Development Company Ltd (COBDC). They were a China based contractor. So, this job offered me completely new experiences – a Chinese style of management, working in Mandarin language and as a civil engineering contractor. I was stationed at their headquarters and assisted in the project management of 12 contracts. As it happened, I only stayed for four months (March-June 1985). Through ICE's newsletter, I applied for a teaching post at Nanyang Technological Institute (NTI) in Singapore and I received an offer in April 1985.

Although I only worked at COBDC for four short months, one significant connection happened. At that time, maybe due to the job situation, I was keen to get more professional qualifications. There was one qualification offered by the American Society of Civil Engineers. Since Hong Kong was a British colony, most engineers would get the British and not the American qualification. So, in Hong Kong, there were very few engineers who were members of the American Society of Civil Engineers (ASCE). However, at COBDC, there was one colleague, George Cheng, who was a member. But to apply for the ASCE membership, I needed two ASCE members to support me. Then, I recalled Dr. Ian McFeat-Smith, a former colleague at Haswell, who was also a member. I asked two of them to support my application, and I became an ASCE member on 1 August 1985. At the time, this appeared to be a total non-event. Nearly two decades later, this proved to be a highly significant milestone in my entire life!

Having worked for a consultant and a contractor, I could see that the job could never be stable as it was dependent on the companies getting new contracts. Looking for a more stable working environment, the offer by NTI looked appealing. First, NTI was an academic institute supported by the Singapore government. Second, the job was to conduct teaching at university level, which should have long-term prospects. After discussing with my wife Christina, she was more than willing to support my move. She was even prepared to resign from her job in Hong Kong and accompany me to Singapore. With such grand support, I accepted NTI's offer. Incidentally, I could also see why there was that four working months at COBDC, so that I didn't feel I was "forced" to move out of Hong Kong.

On 8 July 1985, Christina and I left Hong Kong for the little red dot, Singapore.

Chapter 3

Academic years

Without any professional teaching and research experiences, I stepped into the academic world. I joined Nanyang Technological Institute (NTI) on 9 July 1985. NTI was a new tertiary institute set up by the Singapore government in 1981. At that time, it conducted three engineering courses up to the Bachelor degree level. Since NTI was a new institute, they had the arrangement for their graduates to receive their degrees from the other more established university, National University of Singapore (NUS). Hence, the students from both NTI and NUS received the same degrees. Upon joining the School of Civil and Structural Engineering at NTI as a senior lecturer, I had no idea whether I would like working as an academic and also living in a foreign country Singapore. In any case, I had the contingency plan that if I didn't like it, I could always go back to Hong Kong to practice engineering after the 3-year contract at NTI.

As it happened, I loved working at NTI and living in Singapore. There are several reasons why I like Singapore more than Hong Kong. First, the common language in Singapore is English while it is Cantonese in Hong Kong. After years of living in UK, my English is more fluent than my Cantonese. Second, the Singapore town planning is really superb. It is even better than some of the cities in Europe. I used to joke with my visitor friends that they would never find a traffic jam in Singapore, and also never see a policeman on a street because it was so crime free. But I can't say the same joke in the 2010s. So, the Singapore living conditions are far superior to those of Hong Kong. In fact, when we first arrived at NTI, the staff quarters provided to my wife and I was two to three times bigger than my apartment in Hong Kong. Third, Singaporeans appeared to be less materialistic than Hong Kongers, which of course appealed to my spiritual nature. But I am not sure if I can say the same about Singaporeans in the 2010s, as they seem to have been converted to Moneytheism and craving for the 5Cs (cash, car, condominium, credit card and country club). Fourth, Singapore was very affordable at that time. Even on my lecturer salary, my family and I could enjoy luxurious dining in 5-star hotels every week.

Unfortunately, many of these points are not applicable to Singapore today in 2016. Nowadays, we eat at hawker centres. Not that there is anything wrong with eating at hawker centres, but the quality of life has definitely dropped. In fact, for the years 2014-2016, according to the surveys by the Economist Intelligence Unit (EIU), Singapore has been ranked the most expensive city in the world. You see how much Singapore has changed over the period of 30 years, and one may not necessarily say it's for the better. It very much depends on which side of the divide you are on, and I don't mean the physical divide (geographical location). I mean the rich-poor divide and the powerful-powerless divide. As Bernie Sanders said "The middle-class is disappearing." This may not be happening only in USA, but also in Singapore.

Regarding the academic work, I found it much more scholarly and intellectually satisfying than practical engineering. I was also fortunate that NTI had a programme to ease the new lecturers into teaching. At that time, NTI prided itself in offering practice-oriented courses. Because of this, they were recruiting practical engineers into teaching. Since some of these engineers, like myself, may not have had prior teaching experience, they had a programme to help the new lecturers. Under the programme, the new lecturers would only take tutorials and laboratory classes in the first year of employment. They would also sit in the lectures to pick up tips on teaching from the more experienced lecturers or professors. Then, in the second and subsequent years, they may also give lectures. This programme helped me a lot to transition from an engineer to a lecturer. Even though at first I was apprehensive in taking a class, I actually enjoyed it right from the start.

There was another reason why it was good teaching in a Singapore tertiary institute. In Singapore, all male citizens and second-generation permanent residents had to go through a military training, commonly known as the National Service (NS), prior to entering university. At that time, the duration of NS was two-and-a-half years, and due to improvements in training and technology, it was subsequently shortened to two years in 2005. What this meant was that the male students in NTI were older and more mature than the university students in other countries. For NTI at that time, there was yet another reason why it was good to teach there. There was a group of polytechnic students who have graduated with a diploma and aspired to earn a university degree. Due to a variety of reasons, they were not able to enter the only local university at the time, NUS, or an overseas university to further their study. So, when NTI started, the students really treasured the opportunity given to them by NTI and they savored the learning experience. So, during my initial years in NTI, the students were so eager to learn, and for us the new lecturers, we were so eager to teach. It was truly a win-win, harmonious relationship.

On top of the harmonious lecturer-student relationship, at that time, the School was very well managed by the Prof. Chen Charng-Ning who was the Dean of School (equivalent to Head of Department). So, the management-staff relationship was also harmonious. Since NTI was a new institute, the relationships among staff were also amicable. In fact, this was a great strength of NTI. Every staff member was willing to put in extra as long as it was good for NTI. My own relationship with students was a simple teaching relationship. My relationship with the management was a simple administrative relationship. My relationship with colleagues was a simple academic relationship. There was no need for any wheeling and dealing, or even networking. I just did my teaching and my other work in my office. Over the years, I taught the basic courses: Fluid Mechanics, Hydraulics, Hydrology, and the more advanced courses: Surface Water Hydrology, Urban Hydrology and Water Resources Engineering. I loved the working environment and it was truly a great time working in NTI. You see without the "nasty" contractor and without being fired by Haswell, would I get to experience this wonderful life?

As I was so happy with the job during my first year in NTI, I decided to make it a long-term stay in Singapore. How long? After 30 years, I am still here. On 23 January 1986, I gave up my expatriate status (read foreign talent), and became a permanent resident of Singapore. On 31 August 1990, I even became a Singapore citizen (read local untalent). My wife also joined me to become a permanent resident and then a Singapore citizen. On the job front, I was also interested to make it a career. To pursue an academic career in a university, the normal academic qualification is a doctorate (PhD) degree, which I didn't have. Hence, I approached NTI to see if I could study part-time for a PhD degree and work as a full-time lecturer. Actually, at that time, NTI was more focused on teaching and had not really started on research. I did not expect them to agree. However, beyond my expectation, they agreed to my suggestion. In July 1986, while working as a member of the academic staff in NTI, I enrolled as a PhD candidate with NUS.

Even during those early academic years, while I was learning the ropes of teaching, it was not all academic work. In 1987, I found time to train for the 42 km Mobile Marathon, which I completed on 20 December 1987 in 5 hours and 45 minutes.

Back to the academic work, during my second year in NTI, my research started along with the heavier teaching load. As it happened, I also loved my research. As academic staff members, we were supposed to do research anyway. In fact, in many universities, the priority for an academic staff is first research and second teaching. This is because for any university to be considered as a top university, it is important for their academic staff to conduct outstanding research. I was also fortunate to have Prof. Chen, Dean of my School, as my PhD supervisor. I was therefore doing research as an academic staff member and using it for my PhD degree. So, even though I was supposed to be working full-time and studying part-time, the work was manageable as there wasn't any conflict of interest. In fact, what it meant was that I was more conscious and serious with my research. For the PhD research, I worked on the topic *"Assessment of Flood Peak Increase due to Urbanization"*. There were experimental work and analytical formulations of flow on an overland plane, and computer simulations of an idealized catchment and a natural catchment. I gladly did them all. Since the duties of academic staff naturally came first (since I was paid to do them), the PhD research took a back seat. Eventually, after a long seven years, I submitted and defended my thesis *"Assessment of Flood Peak Increase due to Urbanization"* in 1993. This was just before I went for my 8-month sabbatical leave (27

September 1993-27 May 1994) in UK. And while I was in UK, on 22 April 1994, I received the letter from NUS informing me that my thesis was accepted for the PhD degree. It was of course a great joy to receive the news but there was also a strange feeling. I worked for the degree for so many years in Singapore and yet, when I received the good news, I was not in Singapore but in UK. From that day onwards, I could put the title "Dr." before my name. So, I became Dr. Tommy Wong. This was of course always my father's wish. His wish has finally come true, but two years after he left his body for the spirit world. Still, I'm sure he was aware and celebrated the good news – in good spirit. Upon returning to Singapore from my sabbatical leave, my family and I attended my convocation on 3 September 1994.

While I was pursuing the academic qualification PhD, I was in fact also pursuing my professional qualifications. Being third time lucky, I eventually passed England's professional examination and became a "Chartered Engineer" on 1 December 1988. About one year later, I also passed Singapore's professional examination and became a "Professional Engineer" on 9 February 1990. To cap my professional career, in 1996, I was invited to be listed in "*Who's Who in Science and Engineering*", and in 1998, I was listed in "*Who's Who in the World*". I was also listed in some of their subsequent editions and other Who's Who publications. In July 1999, I was elected to become a fellow of ASCE. All these are very high honors indeed, which I never dreamt of achieving.

In addition to the academic and professional qualifications that I was pursuing, I was in fact also busy on another front - adding members to my family. Christina and I are blessed with three wonderful sons – Alston in 1988, Lester in 1990, and Hanson in 1993. They have all become fine young men today in 2016.

Now back to NTI which continued to evolve. In 1991, NTI merged with the National Institute of Education (NIE) to form Nanyang Technological University (NTU). So, NTU became the second university in Singapore and awarded their own degrees. In 1996, Prof. Chen stepped down as the Dean of School, and a new management team took over. I would say Prof. Chen did an excellent job in building the School and left it in a pretty good shape. In 2001, to give more prominence to the environmental research in the School, the School name was changed to "School of Civil and Environmental Engineering".

Among all these happenings, there was another major happening. In 1999, NTU decided to convert the titles of the academic staff so that it was more in line with the universities in USA and some of the other overseas universities. Previously, the academic staff was designated into four grades:

Professor, Associate professor, Senior lecturer and Lecturer. These designations were then converted into three grades: Professor, Associate professor and Assistant professor. With the new designations, one benefit is that everybody is a professor. So, for the professors and associate professors under the "old" designations, they retained their respective titles under the "new" designations. The real benefactors of the conversion were the senior lecturers under the "old" designations. For the senior lecturers who were on the super-scale (a salary scale with significantly higher pay), they were "upgraded" to become associate professors under the "new" designations. The lecturers under the "old" designations basically took the title assistant professor under the "new" designations. I was already on the super-scale in 1989. So, I was one of the benefactors and got "promoted" to associate professor. I became Associate Professor Tommy Wong or Prof. Wong in short. Throughout my career, I never had a promotion. This was my only "promotion" and it wasn't even real.

Taking a comparison of the two designation systems, I would say the old system was better. For a young academic staff member joining NTU, he would start as a lecturer. He had to perform to be promoted to senior lecturer. He then had to continue to perform to be promoted to the super-scale. He then really had to perform to be promoted to associate professor. Finally, his performance had to be outstanding in order to be promoted to professor. So, there was something to work for throughout the academic's career. On the other hand, under the new system, a young academic staff member joining NTU, he would start as an assistant lecturer. If he performs, he would be promoted to associate professor and super-scale at the same time. After that, there was only the professor grade to work towards. Since not everybody and not many can be promoted to professor, some associate professors may feel there would be no more career advancement. So, after being promoted to associate professor, apart from interest or advancement to other universities, there may be nothing else to work for.

As an academic, it is important to publish papers. As the common saying goes: "Publish or perish". In 1987, Prof. Chen and I published our first conference paper *"Comparison of Kinematic Wave and Rational Methods for Site Drainage Design"*. In 1992, I published my first discussion paper in an academic journal *"Discussion of Physically Based Flood Features and Frequencies"*. In 1993, Prof. Chen and I published our first journal paper *"Critical Rainfall Duration for Maximum Discharge from Overland Plane"*. These are significant steps forward. In the academic world, they see conference publications and journal publications quite differently. Since a conference is an academic as well as a social, networking occasion, it is therefore much easier to have a paper accepted by a conference for publication. On the other hand, for a journal to be recognized as a top journal, it has to maintain a certain academic standard. Also, all the top academics around the world submit their papers to journals for publication, and clearly, the journals will only publish papers of highest quality. These journals tend to be international and not local. Hence, the competition to publish in international journals is intense. Because of this, when universities consider promotion or tenureship of their staff, they may only consider international journal publications. This is another reason why it is so hard to get a paper published in journals. On the other hand, because of the keen competition, it is a prestige to be an author of a published journal paper, and the academic enjoys a higher, academic standing. So, in 1992, I have joined the ranks of published journal author. Appendix A contains a list of my publications in international journals.

When I was completing and near the end of my PhD research, I started to pursue my own individual research without supervision. In 1994, I published my first single-author journal paper *"Kinematic Wave Method for Determination of Road Drainage Inlet Spacing"*. Thereafter, I published many more single-author papers. Only occasionally, did I join my colleagues or students to publish joint-author papers. During that period, I have developed many analytical formulas and they have been named after me. Can you imagine that there are Wong's formulas in the literature? The more significant formulas developed by Prof. Chen and I are as follows.

In 1993, in the paper "*Critical Rainfall Duration for Maximum Discharge from Overland Plane*", Prof. Chen and I reported the formula which can estimate the concentration time of flow on an overland plane including the effect of flow regime. In 2005, in the paper "*Assessment of Time of Concentration Formulas for Overland Flow*", I showed that by comparing with eight other formulas, the Chen and Wong (1993) formula is the best or one of the best time of concentration formulas.

In 1995, in the paper "*Time of Concentration Formulae for Planes with Upstream Inflow*", I reported the formula which can estimate the concentration time of flow on an overland plane with a flow entering the upstream end of the plane. This is a major breakthrough as no previous formulas can account for the effect of an upstream inflow on the concentration time. In 1996, in the paper "*Time of Concentration and Peak Discharge Formulas for Planes in*

Series", I extended the Wong (1995) formula
to a flow on a series of overland planes. In
2001, in the paper "*Formulas for Time of
Travel in Channel with Upstream Inflow*", I
reported formulas which can estimate the
travel time of flow in an open channel with a
flow entering the upstream end of the
channel. In 2002, in the paper "*Use of
Resistance Coefficients Derived from Single
Planes to Estimate Time of Concentration of
Two-Plane Systems*", I extended the Wong
(1996) formula to become an even more
general time of concentration formula. It
can basically estimate the concentration
time of overland flow for all types of
practical conditions. Finally, in 2009, in the
paper "*Evolution of Kinematic Wave Time of
Concentration Formulas for Overland Flow*", I
reported a summary of the key time of
concentration formulas; some of them have
been developed by me.

While it is difficult to publish papers in journals,
it is even more difficult to win awards for papers
that have been published in journals. In 2004, I won
the J. C. Stevens Award given by ASCE for my
2003 paper "*Discussion of Predicting River Travel
Time from Hydraulic Characteristics*". There are
many rules that govern how this award can be

awarded. The following two are the most relevant to my situation:

- The award is given to the best discussion of a paper over a 12-month period in the field of hydraulics, including fluid mechanics and hydrology.

- At least one of the authors of the paper is a member of ASCE.

Now you see the important connections to George Cheng of COBDC and Dr. Ian McFeat-Smith of Haswell back in the 1980s in Hong Kong. Without them, I would not become a member of ASCE and therefore would not be eligible for the award. So, I was indeed blessed by the Great Spirit to have the "right" connections.

Now back to the award. Wow! I won the award against all the leading academics in the field of hydraulics worldwide. Also, as this award dates back to 1944, among the winners, there are many who are considered as legends. Some of them are Thomas R. Camp, Donald R. F. Harleman, and John S. McNown. Can you imagine that my name has been listed together with these legends?

At that time, I was also very interested to voluntarily contribute to the work of journals - not just as an author but also as a reviewer of papers and as an editor. Since 1998, I have reviewed papers for the following international journals:

1. Advances in Environmental Research
2. Advances in Water Resources
3. ASCE Journal of Environmental Engineering
4. ASCE Journal of Hydraulic Engineering
5. ASCE Journal of Hydrologic Engineering
6. ASCE Journal of Irrigation and Drainage Engineering
7. ASCE Journal of Professional Issues in Engineering Education and Practice
8. Hydrological Processes
9. Hydrological Sciences Journal
10. Journal of Hydroinformatics
11. Journal of Hydrology
12. The Open Civil Engineering Journal
13. The Open Hydrology Journal
14. Urban Water Journal
15. Water Science and Technology

On the editorial front, in 2004 and 2007, I was invited to join the editorial boards of the journals *"Advances in Water Resources"* and *"The Open Civil Engineering Journal"*, respectively. In 2006 and 2007, I joined the *"Journal of Professional Issues in Engineering Education and Practice"* as a corresponding editor, and the "*Journal of Hydrologic Engineering*" as an associate editor, respectively. The latest appointment of becoming an associate editor was actually quite prestigious. For an international academic journal, the editorial board is usually led by one or sometimes two to three editors. They are then supported by a team of associate editors. The associate editors are to help the editors to secure reviews of papers and to make recommendations whether to accept the papers for publication. These recommendations are significant because except for some special cases, the editor would normally follow the recommendations. Since these editors have the authority to accept or reject papers, their decisions have an influence on the future of the profession, and also on the career of the academics who submitted the papers. Although it is volunteer work, there is a significant responsibility. As such, usually only leaders of that academic specialty are admitted to become editors or associate editors. Further, these editors are usually selected from academics all over the world. For those who become editors of a journal, they can be considered as world leaders of that specialty. I was indeed honored to become such an associate editor.

The year 2004 was indeed my glory year. I won the J. C. Stevens Award. I was invited to join the editorial board of the prestigious journal "*Advances in Water Resources*". I was also an invited speaker at the "*International Symposium on Urban Water Cycle in Cheonggyecheon Watershed*" in South Korea. At the symposium, I presented the paper "*Physically Based Approach in Urban Hydrology - How Useful is the Approach?*"

So, I became a university professor, an associate editor, an invited speaker and won an international journal award. I would say it's not bad for a below average primary and secondary school student, and for somebody who only received his PhD degree at a mature age of 42. All these achievements were beyond my wildest dreams. I am truly a late bloomer. For all these achievements to manifest on the physical plane within my present incarnation, I am grateful to the Great Spirit. From this point onwards, I thought I could go from strength to strength. But it wasn't to be.

In 2007, NTU decided to carry out a massive exercise to review the performance of all the professors. At that time, a professor could be working on a 3-year contract or a tenure contract which is a contract up to the age of 55 (commonly referred to as the "T55 contract"). The objective of the exercise was to extend the age limit of the tenure contract from 55 to 65 (commonly referred to as the "T65 contract"). The reasoning behind the extension was that with a longer tenure contract, the professors would be more dedicated to do their work in NTU as their employment was secured till the age of 65. Indeed, it was a massive extension of the tenure contract. In terms of a professor's salary, a 10-year extension means millions of dollars. With this amount of money, for a professor who secures the T65 contract, it should mean no more financial worry for the rest of his life. So, he could happily enter retirement at 65. On the other hand, for a professor who doesn't secure the T65 contract, it could mean leaving NTU. At 55, it would not be easy to find a job in the same or in a new career or to start a business. So, he may struggle for the rest of his life. As the outcome of the exercise could have such extreme opposite impacts on the professors' lives, the earlier harmonious working relationships among staff simply disappeared. Since I was dedicated working for NTU throughout the years and just won the international award in 2004, three years before the exercise, I was confident that I would get the T65 contract. And the exercise had a first round and a second round. So, on 9 May 2007, it was a bombshell when I heard that I was eliminated in the first round. To say I was devastated would be truly an under-understatement. When I reached home that day, I could see that my research effort of more than two decades just evaporated. Soon I could be out of the work and all this effort wouldn't bring in a penny. What was I to do?

As it happened, even though I didn't get the T65 contract, NTU offered me a one-and-a-half year contract followed by another one-year contract. So, two-and-a-half years after the exercise, and 25 years after joining NTU, on 25 June 2010, I walked out of my office for the last time. The world in front of me looked so bleak. I had no idea how the rest of my life would unfold. Unfold it did. As I drove out of NTU for what I thought would be the last time and that I would never return. Yet, I did return.

Chapter 4

From an engineering professor to a spiritual author

Engineering and spirituality are two ends of a spectrum which ranges from the physical to the non-physical. Scientists and engineers work at the physical end in which scientists endeavor to find out the physical laws and engineers apply these laws supposedly to make the world better in the physical dimension. If the physical environment improves, generally the mental and the emotional aspects of humans also become better. Traditionally, religionists work at the spiritual end with the endeavor to find out the spiritual laws. They then apply and share these laws with the population supposedly to make the world better in the spiritual dimension. If the spiritual aspects of humans improves, generally the mental and the emotional aspects of humans also become better. It can be said that engineering endeavors to improve the outer world while spirituality endeavors to improve the inner world. From this perspective, engineering and spirituality share a common objective. However, there are fundamental differences in their approaches. When scientists are finding out the physical laws, they generally use scientific instruments to collect data of the physical phenomena. They are observable, repeatable and rational. On the other hand, when religionists are finding out the spiritual laws, they generally rely on spiritual phenomena that are written in books by spiritual masters. Hence, they may not be observable, repeatable or rational. The religious practice is said to be based on good faith. As such, some scientists such as Richard Dawkins have great difficulties with religions. This is also why engineering and spirituality seldom intertwine.

In 1992, completely unplanned and unknowingly, I stumbled into a mind control workshop in which they taught the alpha meditation. It was most strange that I ended up in this type of workshop as I was a rational-minded engineer and researcher. During the workshop, they even taught a type of spirituality which is non-religious. It is sometimes referred to as new age or new thought spirituality. Its practice is love based, experiential and there is no one fixed doctrine. There is no one organization controlling all the followers, no one book that everyone must follow, and no one place that everybody must go. This is so different from organized religions. I found it so refreshing. Many of the concepts and practices expounded by the teacher also made sense to me. So, while I never felt comfortable with any of the religious teachings and practices, I felt very comfortable with this type non-religious spirituality. Since many people may not be clear on the differences between these two types of spirituality, there is a clarification in Chapter 9. Even after the 1992 workshop, I continued to explore both types of spirituality by attending many more talks, seminars, and workshops. I also read many books on both types of spirituality. For the non-religious spirituality, I particularly like the books by Dr. Wayne Dyer and Neale Donald Walsch. Gradually, I was leaning more and more towards the non-religious.

At that time, as I had a comfortable job at the university, I was learning all this spirituality as a hobby. Little did I know that one day I would use it to make a living. In any case, I felt very comfortable with engineering and spirituality and did not see them as conflicting. In fact, when I do work in engineering and spirituality, I find that my engineering background strengthens my spiritual work, and vice versa. There is definite synergy between the two. My engineering enables me to rationalize spirituality, and my spirituality enables me to practice engineering with heart and soul.

Further, there is one fundamental reason why I am keen to do spiritual work. It is apparent that there are many problems in the world. What is the source of these problems? I would say it is in the human spirit. If this is so, then engineering can never solve them because the problems are spiritual and non-physical. In fact, it is not difficult to find places that are beautiful physically, and yet, lack the human spirits. Singapore being a classic example. Oh, why Singapore? It holds the world record in detaining a human being without trial. Dr. Chia Thye Poh was detained for 23 years and subsequently under house arrest for another nine years. To solve the world's problems at the root, I believe we need a shift in spirituality and this is where the non-religious spirituality comes in. So, having been involved with non-religious spirituality for decades, I have always wanted to help the world by doing spiritual work. For many years well before I left NTU, I had always asked when I could start my spiritual work. At that time, it seemed that it would never happen. With the grace of the Great Spirit, it happened. I could also see why I was at the 1992 workshop. The Great Spirit was preparing me for a spiritual career. So, on 9 May 2007, when I knew that I did not get the T65 contract and my days in NTU were numbered. I thought it might be a good opportunity to start my spiritual work, but how?

In modern day spirituality, there was a great spiritual master – his name is Sathya Sai Baba.

Even in the 1992 workshop, he was mentioned by the teacher. After the workshop and in my subsequent spiritual explorations, I learned much more about Sai Baba. On 1 August 2003, I went to the Sai Center at Moulmein Road in Singapore and joined their bhajan (devotional singing) session for the first time. At that time, their practice attracted me because they were supposed to be non-religious. During the bhajan session, it was mostly singing and there was very little time spent on sermon. As such, it was very unimposing and I felt comfortable with the proceedings. So, after the first visit, I became a regular at the bhajan session. Through my interactions with the Sai devotees, I learned even more about Sai Baba. At that time, I had always wanted to go to India to see Sai Baba. In 2005, I had the chance and it was my first visit. Thereafter, I went six more times on an annual basis until his passing in 2011. So altogether, I have visited Sai Baba seven times.

Towards the end of 2008, one evening after dinner, while I thought I would just relax, somehow I went to my study and had the inspiration to write a book. The book would be about my experience with Sai Baba. As it was not my plan to write the book, I sat in front of my computer and didn't know what to write. Then somehow, the writing started. The writing process continued and the first draft was completed in May 2009. In the process of writing, very often, I received the inspiration in the middle of the night. I would even feel something bulging and wanting to come out of my head. This made me very uncomfortable and therefore I had to get up. Since I could not sleep, I proceeded to turn on my computer and started writing. Usually, the writing which came through this way was very good – better than those written in the "normal" daytime. After being "forced" to write in the middle of the night a few times, I got smart by leaving the computer on. So, when the inspiration came, I would simply go to my computer and start writing. When the manuscript was completed, I started to look for a publisher, but could not find any who would accept my manuscript. Then, through inspiration, I found CreateSpace – a self-publishing arm of Amazon. On 9 September 2009, my first spiritual book *"How Sai Baba Attracts without Direct Contact"* was published. It included my spiritual journey from birth and my first five visits to see Sai Baba. So, completely unplanned and unprepared, I have become a spiritual book author.

If you think it's a miracle that I have a spiritual book under my name, the miracle did not end there. Publishing a book produced by CreateSpace has one big advantage. It is available on the world's biggest online bookstore Amazon.com at a very low cost. However, by having the book on Amazon doesn't mean it can sell because it is competing with more than 10 million other books. Further, being an unknown rookie spiritual book author and with an engineering background, the book really should not be able to sell. Miraculously, the book sold. In fact, at that time, the sale of the book was not too far behind even compared to the other classic books on Sai Baba, such as *"Man of Miracles"* by Howard Murphet, and *"Sai Baba – The Ultimate Experience"* by Phyllis Krystal. By this stage, my entire venture into spiritual writing was already gratifying. As it happened, there was more to come, a lot more to come!

Having published my first book on Sai Baba, I really thought it would be the only book that I would write about Sai Baba. In any case, the book included my first five visits to see Sai Baba, which took five years to happen. So, even if there was a second book, I thought it would take at least another five years so as to gather enough material to write the book. In spirituality, miracles happen most unexpectedly. On 8 February 2011, during my seventh visit, I spiritually received a message from Sai Baba that I would be writing a second book. During that visit, he gave me so much material (experience) that it was indeed enough to write the book. So, after the visit, I started my writing in earnest and the second book *"How Sai Baba Attracts without Direct Contact (Book 2)"* was published on 23 May 2011 – less than two years after the first book was published.

In fact, while I was writing my second Sai Baba book, Sai Baba was very sick and he finally left his physical body on 24 April 2011. It was indeed no coincidence that Sai Baba "invited" me to see him in February 2011 – only two months before his passing. It was also no coincidence that he prompted me to write the two books as the main message in the books is to make spiritual connection with him. Soon after his passing, on several websites, a list of public followers of Sathya Sai Baba has been posted. The list is in Appendix B and my name is on it.

A couple of years later, one day in February 2013, while I was casually browsing the internet and not expecting to find anything significant, yet I found that my two Sai Baba books have been listed on the "*Sathya Sai Baba*" page and other pages on Wikipedia. The books have been listed under "*Further reading*" and there are only ten books on the list. Apart from my books, all the other books can be considered as classic books on Sai Baba. I mean there are hundreds of books on Sai Baba and yet my books are among the short list of ten books. Wouldn't you say this is a miracle? So, I have not just become a spiritual book author, but a "famous" spiritual book author. The list of ten books is in Appendix C.

In between the two Sai Baba books, I was in fact doing other spiritual writings. Just as miraculous as the first Sai Baba book, one day in late 2009 out of the blue, an idea came to me that I would write a book on life. What was even more miraculous was that the writing style was not going to be the normal descriptive style but a conversational style. Up to that point in my life, I hadn't written anything remotely close to that style. So with this book, not only did I not know what to write but I also didn't know how to write it but the writing started. On 1 February 2010, I published the book *"Wisdom on How to Live Life"*. In this book, I created three characters – a young man Tom and two gurus, Dick and Harry. The names actually just came from Tom, Dick and Harry. The two gurus, Dick and Harry, have completely opposite philosophies of life. Guru Dick epitomizes someone from a worldly society who emphasizes on the importance of money and power. Guru Harry epitomizes someone from a spiritual society who considers peace and love are more important. In the book, Tom has a conversation with Guru Dick followed by a conversation with Guru Harry to discuss essentially the same questions about life. Since the two gurus have opposite life philosophies, they therefore offer contrasting answers. The book is a satire. The conversational style was used to effectively show the folly of Guru Dick and the wisdom of Guru Harry. After the book was published, the content and the writing style were well received, as demonstrated by the Judge's commentary from the 18th Annual Writer's Digest International Self-Published Book Awards Competition:

> This was a wonderful, thought changing book. I thought the author did a wonderful job of using the conversations between the two Gurus and Tom to teach the lesson of the book. I was very impressed with the easy of reading such complex ideas. Dr. Wong used 'real-life' examples, I could almost picture who Guru Dick was (I have met many of these types) and the same for Guru Harry (I only hope to know more people like this in my life). The story Dr. Wong tells has helped me to inspire to be a better person in everything I do.

Indeed, to put the world's problems in a nutshell: there are too many Guru Dicks and too few Guru Harrys. It is also no coincidence that the subtitle of the book is *"Transforming Earth into Heaven"*. Yes, Earth can become Heaven if we all behave like Guru Harry, and this is the main message in the book. After the book was published, I sent one copy to Mr. Tan Kin Lian whom I only knew through his blog. Subsequently, we met and he was willing to help me to promote and sell the book. I was so lucky. With Mr. Tan's help, the book was selling.

After having written one Sai Baba book and one Wisdom book, I really thought that would be the end of my spiritual writing "career". I mean it's not bad for an engineering professor to have written two spiritual books, right? Little did I know it was only the beginning!

Soon after the first Wisdom book was published, I was inspired to write a second. On 1 June 2010, the book *"Wisdom on How to Live Life (Book 2)"* was published. Just as a proof that I was not totally unaware there would be sequels to my first Sai Baba and Wisdom books, in the titles of these two books, there is no mention of "Book 1". But in their sequels, "(Book 2)" is in the titles. As for the Wisdom books, the inspiration continued to come. Typically, the inspiration would only come after the writing of an earlier book had been completed. So, I continued to write my Wisdom books and eventually, I ended up writing a series of five books. *"Wisdom on How to Live Life (Book 3)"* was published on 10 October 2010, *"Wisdom on How to Live Life (Book 4)"* on 11 November 2011, and *"Wisdom on How to Live Life (Book 5)"* on 24 July 2012. The publication of the fifth and last book in the *"Wisdom on How to Live Life"* book series coincide with my 30th wedding anniversary. What a wonderful, loving 30-year marriage with Christina and it is still going strong!

Earlier it was mentioned that I created three characters, the young man Tom, Guru Dick and

Guru Harry, in the book "*Wisdom on How to Live Life*". In fact, only the first book of the book series has all three characters. In the subsequent books, since the books are more focused on the spiritual aspect of life and living, there are only Tom and Guru Harry. However, based on readers' feedback, actually they liked Guru Dick more, probably because of his "twisted" arguments and requested me to bring him back. But the book series has moved on without Guru Dick, so how could I bring him back?

On 9 June 2012, I attended a public forum on "*Minimum Wage – for Low Wage Workers*". There was a panel of five speakers and they discussed whether minimum wage should be implemented in Singapore since Singapore is one of the few countries in the world that doesn't have minimum wage. During the discussions, basically four were for the minimum wage and one was against. After coming home from the forum, I thought that if I wrote a book on the minimum wage, it would be an opportunity to bring Guru Dick back. You see for Guru Dick and Guru Harry to appear in the same book, the book has to cover a topic which has two opposing viewpoints. Eureka! Minimum wage is exactly such a topic. Hence, based on the points raised in the forum, I quickly wrote the little book "*Minimum Wage for Low Wage Workers*", and it was published on 24 July 2012. Also, to show that

Guru Dick is back, the subtitle of the book is *"Conversations between Tom, Guru Dick and Guru Harry"*. I then thought this would be a one-off book. Little did I know, it was actually the beginning of another series. Subsequently, I wrote two more books in this series. They are *"Masters of Life on Meaningful Living"* published on 24 July 2013, and *"Masters of Life on Good Life and Good Society"* published on 14 December 2014. The masters of life are of course Guru Dick and Guru Harry. These two books have now formed part of the *"Masters of Life"* series.

As I get feedback from readers every now and then, another feedback I got was that while *"Wisdom on How to Live Life"* book series is good and interesting, it covers many topics and doesn't appear to have a focus. Also, in terms of marketing, the title appears to be too general. This was indeed good feedback. At the time, I was inspired to choose a general title because it could then cover any topic on life. This was important because I wouldn't know what topics would come through. However, as the entire series has already been published, for marketing purposes, it may be better to use more specific titles for future books. Also, to respond to the readers' feedback, I thought why not? I pulled out extracts from the book series that are related to spiritual living and put them into one book. Subsequent to the publication of *"Minimum Wage for Low Wage Workers"*, I did exactly that. As part of my 60th birthday celebration on 14 December 2012, the book *"Wisdom for Spiritual Living"* was published. On that birthday, I officially entered the world of senior citizens, a grand old man with or without wisdom!

While the book *"Wisdom for Spiritual Living"* can be considered the sixth book in the *"Wisdom on How to Live Life"* book series, it is in fact the beginning of another *"Wisdom"* book series. For the books in this series, there are only Tom and Guru Harry. So, it is different from the books in the *"Masters of Life"* series, which have Tom and the two gurus. So, there are two distinct series: one with Guru Dick and one without Guru Dick. Subsequent to the book *"Wisdom for Spiritual Living"*, I have written four more books in the *"Wisdom"* series. On 9 September 2013, *"Wisdom for End-of-Life Living"* was published. On 1 March 2014, *"Wisdom for Living After Being Fired"* was published. Then, as a sequel to *"Wisdom for Spiritual Living"*, *"Wisdom for Living as Spiritual Beings"* was published on 15 September 2015. Indeed, the subtitle of this book is *"How to Live Spiritually in Non-Spiritual Society"* which is the main work I am doing.

So, by the end of 2015, I have written and published 14 books in the philosophy, self-help and spirituality genres. The book you are reading now is the fifteenth. Wouldn't you say it is not bad for an ex-engineering professor?

Appendix D contains the 14 books in the sequence of publication. As you can see, there is no particular logic to the sequence. This is because all these books came through via inspiration. So, I never know when and which book would come through. I am truly just an instrument to the Great Spirit!

Chapter 5

Care for the dying

After my father's passing on 18 November 1992, my mother was staying alone in Hong Kong. As she was obviously getting old, I thought it would be better if she could stay close to one of her children. Hence, as a preparation for her moving to Singapore, I bought an apartment on her behalf on 20 June 1994. On 22 February 1996, my mother moved into the apartment which is just next to ours. On 27 June 1999, my mother went to Canada to visit my siblings. Unfortunately, during that visit, she broke both her legs and suffered a stroke. On 11 June 2000, when she returned to Singapore, it was obvious that she couldn't stay in a separate apartment on her own anymore. She therefore moved into the Lentor Residence nursing home. Surprisingly, she was happy at Lentor even though she was only staying in a "small" room with one suitcase. This was a major downgrade from her "huge" apartment in Hong Kong with one hundred and one things. While my mother was completely non-religious and non-spiritual, yet the way she accepted the situation was truly spiritual - she could simply let go.

Years passed, and my mother's health also deteriorated. It eventually reached a point when the nursing home could not cope with her anymore. On 5 September 2007, I took the momentous decision to move her to our apartment and stay with us. This was not an easy decision to make as we had three growing children in the apartment, aged 19, 17, and 14. On top of this, soon after my father-in-law's passing on 27 Nov 1995, my mother-in-law had already moved into our apartment. With my mother moving in, we had a party of nine (mother, mother-in-law, my wife and I, three sons and two maids) living under one roof, and two of them were approaching 100 years young. We were truly having a "jolly" good time, and this was a far cry from my carefree days when I was living alone in Bath, England in the 1970s. While it may be obvious that both my mother and mother-in-law were women, the less obvious was that since my wife, Christina, was of the same gender, a lot of the work "naturally" fell on to her. She truly shouldered a heavy burden, for whom I am forever grateful.

While my mother was staying with us, her health was quite okay. At least there was no need for her to be hospitalized. However, on 8 July 2010, due to complications from her diabetes, she was admitted to the St. Luke's Hospital. She was discharged on 14 August 2010, and I thought she had recovered. Little did I know then, it was the first of several hospitalizations and it was also the beginning of the end. Less than two months later, my mother was hospitalized again between 6-9 October 2010 at the Alexandra Hospital. Then, two months later, my mother was hospitalized for a much longer period from 15 December 2010 to 26 February 2011 at the St. Luke's Hospital. During the subsequent review on 22 March 2011, the doctor advised that as a precautionary measure, it would be better for my mother to be hospitalized again. After the review, we returned home to get ready to send my mother to the hospital. She had lunch at home that day and that was her last meal and last time she was in our apartment. Within the one year period, she was hospitalized for the fourth time between 22 March-23 April 2011. She first stayed at the St. Luke's Hospital between 22 March-17 April 2011. Then, on 17 April 2011, she suffered a heart attack and was transferred to the National University Hospital and stayed between 17-23 April 2011. Finally, my mother passed away peacefully on 23 April 2011. In retrospect, I was so blessed to be given the opportunity and responsibility to take care of my mother for the final fifteen years of her life (except for the one year when she stayed in Canada) after my father's passing.

Since my contract at NTU ended on 30 June 2010, during my mother's hospitalizations which started in July 2010, I was free. Hence, I could and did practically spend full-time with my mother. I brought her in and out of the hospitals, accompanied her in the hospitals and also brought her to other out-patient visits. Leaving NTU in June 2010 was not my plan. I had intended to stay for one more year. Yet, if I had stayed according to my plan, do you see what I would have missed out on? I would have completely missed out on the final ten months of my mother's life. Instead, I was so blessed that I could be by her side practically full-time over that period. Do you see how great is the Great Spirit's plan in taking me out of NTU one year earlier than I had planned? There are many things in life that we may plan but the Great Spirit always has a better plan. This is why in spirituality, it is recommended that we surrender to the Great Spirit!

Coming back to my mother, when she was moving in and out of the hospitals, normally we would call an ambulance to transport her. However, during February-March 2010 just before her final hospitalization, I decided to drive my own car to take her for the out-patient visits. My mother was sitting next to me as I was driving. We did not talk much and yet, it was so surreal. Clearly, she had complete confidence in me that I would do the best for her. Talking about love between mother and son, it couldn't have been more real. This was indeed one of my highest human and spiritual experiences!

With my mother's passing, it was not only losing my mother, it was also losing another "job". And then less than two years later after my mother's passing, on 28 July 2012, we received the news from Hong Kong that Commy's wife (my sister-in-law) had been diagnosed with cancer. It was ampullary cancer which had an unfavorable prognosis. The "standard" treatment was to go through a major and potentially life threatening operation which she did on 15 August 2012. Fortunately, the operation was "successful". In view of the situation, my family and I visited my sister-in-law after her operation in August 2012. In January 2013, since Lester had returned to London, four of us (Christina, Alston, Hanson and myself) visited her again. On 26 March 2013, we received the news that the cancer had reached the fourth stage (the terminal stage). So, another relative of mine was reaching her end-of-life. In August 2013, while Lester was back in Singapore, four of us (Alston, Lester, Hanson and myself) visited my sister-in-law again. Then, in 2014, we heard that her conditions had badly deteriorated. Since Christina and I had made arrangement to visit Lester in London in May-June 2014, we decided to visit my sister-in-law between 15–18 May 2014 prior to the

London trip. That was the last time we saw my sister-in-law as she passed away peacefully on 25 May 2014.

In the midst of my sister-in-law's illness, my mother-in-law was also not well. She had been suffering from old age for several months before she was hospitalized between 14-16 October and 2-5 November 2013. During her second period of hospitalization, essentially we were told that she only had weeks if not days left. So, I had two relatives who were at their end-of-life concurrently. On 5 November 2013, we decided to bring my mother-in-law home so that she could pass on there. When Lester in London heard the news, he decided to fly back immediately. He arrived in Singapore on the morning of 7 November 2013. In the afternoon of the same day, my mother-in-law passed away peacefully, with the entire family around her. It was indeed a miracle that Lester came back just in time to be in the presence of my mother-in-law's passing. On the day when my mother-in-law passed on, she was beyond 100 years young, a centenarian, and close to her 101st birthday.

When both of my relatives were going through their end-of-life, I was inspired to write the book *"Wisdom for End-of-Life Living"* sharing the spiritual perspective on dying. Unlike my other books which I usually wrote at a leisurely pace, with this book, I felt the urgency to complete it quickly.

Indeed, on 9 September 2013, the book was published when both of my relatives were still around. This chapter ends with an extract dedicated to my mother-in-law and sister-in-law. May peace be with them and their families!

Tom: And it's better to live in peace rather than sadness when our loved one leaves the body, right?

Harry: That's right, and there is another point about leaving the body.

Tom: What is the point?

Harry: Let us assume that when we were born, we inherited a body in perfect condition.

Tom: Okay, you mean we incarnate into a perfect able body.

Harry: Now if the body has contracted a terminal illness, is the body still in perfect condition?

Tom: Well, based on the definition of illness, the body cannot be in perfect condition.

Harry: How about terminal illness?

Tom: Then, it means that the body is very far from perfect.

Harry: Okay, now let's us take another body which is at an advanced age.

Tom: Okay, you mean a body of old age.

Harry: Is this body in perfect condition?

Tom: Well, due to the aging process, the body is unlikely to be perfect.

Harry: How about a very old body?

Tom: Then, this body is likely to be very far from perfect.

Harry: So, is there a way to make these bodies perfect again?

Tom: Well from the physical perspective, it is difficult if not impossible.

Harry: But then, is there a "better" way to live?

Tom: Well it would be nice if we could live in perfect body again.

Harry: But it is not possible physically, right?

Tom: Nope.

Harry: Then, how about spiritually?

Tom: Okay, what is the spiritual solution?

Harry: Leave the imperfect body and reincarnate into a perfect body.

Tom: Perfect solution.

Harry: Yes Tom, this is a divine way to let us to live in a perfect body again.

Tom: Hallelujah!

Harry: So, do we have to feel sad when somebody leaves an imperfect body?

Tom: No, we can see it as a process for the soul to move on to a perfect body.

Harry: So, does this help you to live in peace when your loved ones leave their bodies?

Tom: Yes Guru Harry, thank you for your enlightening perspective on living and dying.

Chapter 6

Being unemployed

If you are out of a job and doing some writing to earn a few dollars, are you self-employed or unemployed? Technically, if you are not employed by a company and earning a few dollars, you are self-employed. This is one reason why the official unemployment rate in Singapore is so low. In practical terms, if the few dollars you earn are enough to live on, then you can consider yourself self-employed. But if the few dollars you earn is not enough to pay for your three meals a day, even though strictly speaking you are not unemployed, you'll face all the problems of being unemployed.

To say being unemployed is not a pleasant experience is truly an understatement. In reality, it is horrible. There are all kinds of stigma that goes with the unemployed. I mean who likes to be associated with an unemployed? This is perhaps why despite the unpleasantness and the situation really needs support from friends and families, some would hide it from their families. For others, they would hide it from their friends by telling them that they are self-employed or retired. This makes them more respectable, and they are right. I mean who respects an unemployed? After I left NTU, I became unemployed. In fact to strangers, I may do the same as the other unemployed which is pretending that I was self-employed or retired. However, to the people I know or so called "friends", I would tell them the truth. I am not proud of my employment status but at the same time, I am not ashamed.

For somebody who lost his job, you may have heard that even though he found another job, his pay was much lower. He may lament to you that he couldn't find a job that matched his previous pay and his income has dropped by 50%. He may even share with you that he had to make lots of adjustments to live on this lower income and life is terrible. What this person shared with you is true! Life is terrible when income drops by 50%. On the other hand, things could be worse. For another person, he may lose his job and can't find another job. He would then live without a job and remain jobless. What happens to his income? In an affluent country like Singapore, unless you are really, really poor, basically penniless, the government gives you nothing. If you are really penniless, the government may give you a few hundred dollars each month to keep you going or not going as the case may be. There is basically no social safety net in Singapore –

no money for the unemployed. The idea is to encourage (or force) everybody to work for his own living. The theory is that there are plenty of jobs in Singapore and everybody is employable. This is why you can see old folks in their seventies still working as cleaners in hawker centers. So, if you are not prepared to work as a cleaner and choose to be an unemployed in Singapore, your income drops by 100%. Then, what happens to those who for whatever reason, cannot work or cannot find a job? Hard luck, my friend. As the saying goes "You die is your business". Singapore isn't a welfare state, period. And don't talk about humanity in Singapore. Remember it holds the world record for detaining a fellow human being without trial. So, welcome to a totally elitist, materialistic and non-spiritual society. No wonder in Singapore, the rich are getting richer and the poor are getting poorer. Also, no wonder the Great Spirit "sent" me here to do spiritual work. After I left NTU, I couldn't find a job and became unemployed. What do you think is the percentage drop in my income?

I was lucky. My income did not drop by 100%. The Great Spirit had prompted me to write and publish books prior to leaving NTU, and my books could sell. So, I got income from my books. This was a great boost to my self-esteem as I could tell everybody that I was still earning. I have no doubt that this was the Great Spirit's plan. So, what do you think is the percentage drop in my income? My monthly pay at NTU was in five figures. After leaving NTU, my monthly income from selling my books was one or two digits. You may think this income is low but actually, it is not bad for an "unknown" author like me. It could easily have been zero. So, the drop in income was more than 99%. If life is terrible when the income drops by 50%, can you imagine what life is like when it drops by 99%? Yes, I know it is hard to imagine, especially for those who have a job and a steady income. I suppose it is equally hard for people with a good income to imagine what life is like for people with low or no income. No wonder for the million-dollar Singapore ministers (highest paid ministers in the world), it is so difficult for them to understand the plights of ordinary Singaporeans. For me, I have the "good fortune" to experience life on a low income. As part of that experience, I have found a way to save ten cents. There are two coffee shops near my home, and one of them is slightly farther away but sells tea at ten cents cheaper. Guess which one I patronize when I go for my tea? Yes, you may laugh at the "insignificant" saving, but if your income is a few dollars, ten cents is a big saving! There was another reason for me to save. I didn't expect to find a job with a decent income ever again in my present incarnation. But I did. So, for all practical purposes, I was unemployed. Yet nearly all the people around me were either retired or gainfully employed. So, they all thought I had no financial problems or simply no problems. For the unemployed, where will money come from? Maybe it will fall from the sky. Or maybe like Sai Baba, it can be materialized through thin air. Anyway, for the unemployed, money is only one of the many problems - a thin end of a really thick wedge. For whatever reasons, I experienced most of them. Through this experience, I would like to think that I have become a more humane human, and a more enlightened soul. In my book *"Wisdom for Living After Being Fired"*, I have highlighted the problems and offered a spiritual solution. The following is the extract on the problems:

Harry: After you've lost your job, you would also lose your income, right?

Tom: Yes, no more income.

Harry: The next thing you'll lose is your colleagues.

Tom: You mean they'll become ex-colleagues.

Harry: Actually, it's worse than that.

Tom: What do you mean?

79

Harry: They won't want to know you anymore.

Tom: But we had been colleagues for decades.

Harry: Does it matter?

Tom: How can that be?

Harry: You just wait and see.

Tom: But really are there any reasons why they don't want to know me?

Harry: Of course.

Tom: What are the reasons?

Harry: First, you can't bring benefit to them anymore, right?

Tom: Well yes, a bit difficult, at least not financially.

Harry: Second, you have actually become a burden, you know?

Tom: Oh, how about I don't ask them for anything?

Harry: But how can they be sure?

Tom: I see.

Harry: And then you actually need help.

Tom: Yes, I do.

Harry: So, they won't feel comfortable with you around.

Tom: I see again.

Harry: Also they don't know whether to help or not to help.

Tom: You mean I'm putting them in a dilemma?

Harry: And also how to help?

Tom: So it's better for them to alienate me?

Harry: I mean it's not a very nice thing to say, but you are an outcast now.

Tom: So it's more comfortable for them to alienate me.

Harry: And the third reason is that you can't be in the "good" book of the management, right?

Tom: Well, in fact, this is why I was fired.

Harry: Exactly, so it is not to their interest to be associated with you, right?

Tom: You mean the management will know.

Harry: They have eyes everywhere.

Tom: You mean they have ears everywhere.

Harry: I mean it's not worth your ex-colleagues to take the risk, right?

Tom: But I thought we were friends.

Harry: This is in fact the next thing you'll lose.

Tom: What? You mean friends?

Harry: My dear friend, do you understand your situation?

Tom: I suppose not exactly.

Harry: You are now "down and out".

Tom: So?

Harry: Why do you suppose people still want to befriend you?

Tom: Because we are friends.

Harry: This is also exactly why your friends will leave you.

Tom: You mean they are not my "real" friends?

Harry: Yes, those who leave you are not your real friends.

Tom: So my real friends will stay.

Harry: But you may not find anybody there.

Tom: So grim?

Harry: Welcome to the real world, my dear Tom!

Tom: Then, what is the next thing I'll lose?

Harry: Your family.

Tom: What? Impossible.

Harry: *Yes, the impossible happens all the time.*

Tom: This is really hard for me to imagine.

Harry: *Yes, you don't have to imagine it. You will see it for real.*

Tom: You are making me worry.

Harry: *Well, there is a saying you know.*

Tom: What is the saying?

Harry: *When the husband loses his job, the wife will go.*

Tom: So, where will she go?

Harry: *Where the money is.*

Tom: But in the marriage vow, it says "for better and for worse".

Harry: *Yes, but it doesn't say for nothing?*

Tom: You mean I am nothing?

Harry: Do you have a job?

Tom: No.

Harry: Yes, you are nothing.

Tom: So cruel!

Harry: Well Tom, let's be practical.

Tom: You mean no money, no talk.

Harry: Actually, no money, no honey!

Tom: You are really making me worry.

Harry: My dear Tom, let me enlighten you.

Tom: Yes, I really need some enlightenment.

Harry: To be fair to your wife, you had been bringing money to the family, right?

Tom: Yes, I had been supporting the family when I had the job.

Harry: But now you don't have income, right?

Tom: Yes, it's because I've lost my job.

Harry: But your family still has to live, right?

Tom: Yes, they have to live.

Harry: For your family to live, there are expenses, right?

Tom: Yes, you mean they need money to live?

Harry: And you may not be able to get another job soon, right?

Tom: Yes, that may be difficult.

Harry: In fact, your situation may persist indefinitely, right?

Tom: You mean no income indefinitely?

Harry: And you will still have expenses, right?

Tom: You mean I've become a liability?

Harry: Let's face it, Tom, you are not exactly an asset.

Tom: Wow, you've just completely destroyed my self-worth.

Harry: So for a brighter future, it may be better for your wife to look for greener pasture, right?

Tom: You mean richer pasture?

Harry: So, you can't blame her, right?

Tom: No, I can only blame myself.

Harry: That's why I said better be prepared.

Tom: I really thought it wouldn't come to this.

Harry: You know there is another point.

Tom: What is the point?

Harry: All the people around you may think it's your fault?

Tom: You mean it's my fault to lose the job?

Harry: If it's not your fault, then whose fault?

Tom: But I've done nothing "wrong".

Harry: Tell that to your boss.

Tom: In fact, I was doing something "right".

Harry: Like losing your job?

Tom: Yeah, because I would rather lose my job than to lose my soul.

Harry: How much is your soul worth, my dear Tom?

Tom: You mean people don't support the "right" action?

Harry: Is there any money in it?

Tom: Why do you always talk about money?

Harry: Because it's money and power that rule our world.

Tom: But how about friends and family?

Harry: I've told you already.

Tom: You are making me more depressed.

Harry: Actually, it's not me who is making you more depressed.

Tom: Then who?

Harry: Dare I say it, yourself.

Tom: What?

Harry: Well, I mean it's your innocence.

Tom: I know, and you actually mean my ignorance.

Harry: And we haven't come to the end yet.

Tom: You mean after losing my job, colleagues, friends, and family, things can still get worse?

Harry: You may eventually lose yourself?

Tom: My God!

Harry: Yes, you may be going back to Him.

Tom: How?

Harry: Your health may deteriorate mentally or physically or both.

Tom: You mean I'll go insane and kill myself.

Harry: Or you may just kill yourself.

Tom: How can that be?

Harry: Well, after losing your job, colleagues, friends and family, what else do you have left?

Tom: Nothing much.

Harry: And if you can't get another job?

Tom: Yes, the future looks bleak.

Harry: Then, what is there to live for?

Tom: Nothing much, right?

Harry: Then, is life worth living?

Tom: You mean I'm worthless?

Harry: Then, what is an alternative to living?

Tom: You mean dying?

Harry: These scenarios have happened to many in the past.

Chapter 7

Return as consultant

As mentioned in Chapter 5, it was not my plan to leave NTU in June 2010. My plan was to stay for one more year before coming out to do full-time spiritual work. The main motive was to earn one more year's salary which was a six-figure sum as I knew there would be very little money in spiritual work. As it turned out, the earning from my spiritual work was even less than "very little". However, things did not happen according to my plan. I was forced to leave NTU one year earlier which meant that I had earned one year's less salary as compared to my plan. Would it be possible for me to earn that salary back from NTU even though I had already left? If I did, wouldn't you call it a miracle?

In January 2012, during a wedding dinner, I met my ex-colleague Prof. Tan Soon Keat. During our discourse, he mentioned that he had just secured a project in which I could participate if I were interested. Sure, I was interested as I didn't have any job then. A couple of months later, I was invited to attend a meeting on 16 March 2012 at NTU. So, less than two years after I left NTU and I thought that I would never returned, yet I returned. This was the first meeting to kick start the NTU-JTC Corporation (JTC) joint research project *"Empirical Study of Tidal Backwater Effects on Drainage Design at Jurong Island Ayer Chawan Basin"*. This project was right within my specialty. It was also the first project for the newly formed NTU-JTC Industrial Infrastructure Innovation (I^3) Research Centre. See how everything fell into place.

After the first meeting, we started work on the project. While I mainly worked from home, I nevertheless went to NTU on a weekly basis. So, I was back in NTU. On 5 July 2012, I was officially appointed as the consultant to the project. On 28 September 2012, I received my first pay and it was decent. It was approximately half of my full-time salary when I left NTU. The project duration was 12 months. I was exceedingly happy with the arrangement and most grateful to Prof. Tan.

About one year into the project, out of the blue on 25 March 2013, I heard the news that JTC was planning to extend the project for another 10 months. This was unbelievable news. With all the necessary administrative work, the project extension was finally approved and the funding made available on 1 April 2014. This meant that I would receive another 10 months' pay. I therefore received a total of 22 months' pay from the project, which was approximately my one year's full-time salary just before leaving NTU. So, I did earn back that one year salary. In life, sometimes money will chase after us instead of we chase after money.

Further, do you see the great plan by the Great Spirit? It took me out one year earlier so that I could accompany my mother for the last 10 months of her life. Then, it put me back into NTU to earn back that one year salary. How about that for living with the Great Spirit?

Finally, on 28 August 2014, the project was essentially completed as we gave a presentation to JTC on our project report. Thereafter, I went into NTU a few more times for the subsequent meetings and the last one was on 10 September 2014. So, my return to NTU lasted for two years and six months, and the project was successfully completed.

How an engineering professor becomes a spiritual philosopher

Chapter 8

Into politics and socio-political writings

After being fired by NTU, I see the world differently. Before that, you could say I was apathetic to politics. I mean who wants to care about politics when you are having a good life, and I was having a "good" life. But my whole world turned upside down when I lost my job. I could then see how much of our world was controlled by politicians. While we may not want to touch politics, but I can see that politics will always touch us. You may also say that I am spiritual; so how can I be involved in politics? This is the very point I addressed in my book *"Masters of Life on Meaningful Living"*. The following is the extract:

Tom: Okay, apart from helping certain individuals, is there any bigger thing we can do on the outside?

Harry: Sure, we can make the world better.

Tom: How?

Harry: *By becoming chief of a country!*

Tom: Hey Guru Harry, isn't that politics?

Harry: *Yes, is there something wrong with politics?*

Tom: Wow, and this comes from Guru Harry.

Harry: *Yeah, is there something wrong with politics?*

Tom: Well, I've been told that we should not mix spirituality with politics.

Harry: *Well if you do that, isn't that politics in itself?*

Tom: Hmm, you have a point here.

Harry: *And then if we take politics in its broadest sense.*

Tom: Okay, let's take politics in its broadest sense.

Harry: It covers everything, right?

Tom: Right, it covers everything.

Harry: And if we take spirituality in its broadest sense.

Tom: Okay, let's take spirituality in its broadest sense.

Harry: It also covers everything, right?

Tom: Wow sure, it also covers everything.

Harry: So, how can spirituality not mix with politics?

Tom: Or politics mix with spirituality?

Harry: Exactly. So the best place to practice spirituality is actually in politics.

Tom: Fascinating!

Harry: And then there is a saying.

Tom: What is the saying?

Harry: Politics is spirituality demonstrated!

Tom: So, politics is the best place to demonstrate our spirituality.

Harry: And there is another point about spirituality and politics.

Tom: What is the point?

Harry: The practice of spirituality is to help humans to build a "better" society through an inner path.

Tom: How about politics?

Harry: The practice of politics is to help humans to build a "better" society through an outer path.

Tom: So the two paths lead to the same destination?

Harry: Yeap, they actually serve the same purpose.

Tom: Wow, this is mind-blowing!

Harry: You sound surprised?

Tom: Yeah, nobody has put it like this before.

Harry: And there is one more point about spirituality and politics.

Tom: What is the point?

Harry: Spirituality and politics are two main pillars of society, right?

Tom: Sure, they are.

Harry: So, it's better for them to support the same platform, right?

Tom: You mean it's better for them to support the same ideal?

Harry: I mean it's safer for the two pillars to support one platform.

Tom: Rather than for the two pillars to support two different platforms.

Harry: So, it's better for spirituality and politics to work together.

Tom: Rather than for them to work separately.

Harry: Now you see the power of politics with spirituality.

Tom: Yeap, I see that the mix of spirituality with politics can be really powerful.

So, is it such a good idea to be involved in politics? Especially and undoubtedly, politicians are responsible for many atrocities. On the other hand, are they not responsible for many fundamental improvements to societies? Maybe politics can be considered neutral, like a knife in which it can kill or heal depending on how it is being used. And the other point is if we want to do good to society, would it be easier to do it with or without political power? If we don't have political power, how much good can we do? Are we really "good" if we let "bad" people run the country? This point is addressed in my book "*Masters of Life on Good Life and Good Society*". The following is the extract:

Tom: How can we transform Earth into heaven?

Harry: Okay, let's take the first step.

Tom: The very first step.

Harry: First, let "good" people go into politics.

Tom: Hey Guru Harry, we can't do that.

Harry: Oh?

Tom: In our society, "good" people don't go into politics. So, this first step is already very difficult if not impossible.

Harry: Tell me more.

Tom: In our society, we are told that good people shouldn't go into politics.

Harry: Then, who should go into politics?

Tom: "Bad" people.

Harry: So, politics will be full of "bad" people?

Tom: That's right, as you can see for yourself.

Harry: But if only bad people go into politics, will the country be good?

Tom: Nope, the country will be no good.

Harry: So, how can the country be good?

Tom: Let good people go into politics.

Harry: Hmm, I see.

Tom: Oh, this is what you've just said, right?

Harry: Isn't it illogical that people want the country to be good, and yet they let bad people to run the country?

Tom: Guru Harry, you've a point here.

Harry: And for those people who pride themselves to be good.

Tom: Yes.

Harry: If they are not willing to go into politics, are they really good?

Tom: Oh Guru Harry, you've another point here.

Harry: Especially when the country is run by bad people.

Tom: They say they don't want to go in because they don't want to be one of them.

Harry: You mean they are so good?

Tom: Yes, these people have high standards.

Harry: So, they just let bad people ruin the country.

Tom: Hey Guru Harry, these bad people you are referring to are not really bad, you know?

Harry: Oh, tell me more.

Tom: Some people in the country are very prosperous.

Harry: How about the bottom stratum of the society?

Tom: Hmm, we don't talk about them.

Harry: Are they being looked after?

Tom: Well Guru Harry, we all have to look after ourselves.

Harry: So, they are not being looked after.

Tom: I mean they are the bottom stratum of the society.

Harry: And you say they are not bad?

Tom: They are not bad because the rich and powerful are having a good life.

Harry: And the others are having a bad life.

Tom: But since they are not in politics, so it's not their business, you see.

Harry: Yes Tom, would you like to hear a saying?

Tom: What is the saying?

Harry: You don't touch politics, but politics will touch you.

Tom: So, politics will touch us irrespective of whether we are in it or not.

Harry: And without good people running the country, how long can the good life last?

Tom: For the rich and powerful, it can last a long time.

Harry: *And is it really a good life when others are having a bad life?*

Tom: Okay Guru Harry, you don't seem to understand?

Harry: *What do I not understand?*

Tom: The bottom line is good people don't go into politics. Period.

Harry: *Okay, I understand.*

Tom: And there is another point.

Harry: *What is the point?*

Tom: Enlightened people also don't go into politics.

Harry: *Maybe that's why the world is not enlightened.*

Tom: Wow Guru Harry, you have an answer to everything.

Harry: *I have an answer to a better world.*

Tom: Which is?

Harry: Let good people go into politics and run the country.

Tom: Yes, Guru Harry.

Harry: And there is another point.

Tom: What is the point?

Harry: Since all politicians are bad, isn't this a good time for good people to go in?

Tom: You mean isn't this the best time for good people to go in?

Harry: I mean isn't it essential for good people to go in?

Tom: You mean isn't it critical for good people to go in?

Harry: You see if we don't have good leaders, it is difficult to have a good society.

Tom: You mean it is difficult to have a good country.

Harry: I mean it is difficult to transform Earth into heaven.

Tom: So, we don't have a choice but let good people go into politics.

Harry: No Tom, let good people go in by choice.

Tom: So as to create a good society.

Harry: So as to create a better society.

Tom: So as to create a heavenly society.

Harry: So as to bring heaven to Earth.

The year 2011 was a very special election year for Singapore. For the first time in its history, it did not have just one but two major elections. In May 2011, the general election (GE) was held in which the People's Action Party (PAP) returned to power with 60.1% of the popular votes. This is the lowest percentage of votes that PAP had garnered in all the GEs since Singapore's independence. Three months after the GE, the writ for the presidential election (PE) was issued on 3 August 2011. This is an election for Singapore electorates to choose the President of Singapore through the ballot box. Mr.

Tan Kin Lian has decided to stand in this PE. Since Mr. Tan has helped me with the promotion and selling of my books, I thought that I should return the favor and helped him in his election campaign. Also, as I was not working in NTU, I could be freely involved in politics – see another jigsaw in the Great Spirit's plan. It presented to me a golden opportunity to be involved in politics directly. So, not knowing exactly what to expect, I entered the world of politics. I was active throughout the campaign starting even before the nomination day on 17 August 2011. On 24 August 2011, I delivered the following speech at Mr. Tan's election rally.

Good evening, fellow Singaporeans, brothers and sisters, how are you today?

Thank you for coming to Mr. Tan Kin Lian's rally. Thank you for finding time and making an effort to be here. By virtue of the fact that you are here, it shows that you care about Singapore. I salute you.

My name is Tommy Wong. I used to teach at a university as a professor, until I retired from the university last year. I am now a freelance international book author, and have written a series of books with the title 'Wisdom on How to Live Life'. So tonight, I would like to share with you something on life, and something on wisdom which is related to why we should vote wisely in the upcoming Presidential Election. I'll start with the second point first.

On Polling Day, we have a very important decision to make because Singapore's future depends on who will become the next President. And who will become the next President depends on your votes. So your vote is very important.

How many candidates are there in the Presidential Election? Are they all the same? Well, they all have the same surname Tan, but when they become President, they will do things differently. In fact, the four candidates will do things so differently that they will take Singapore to four different directions. And the directions are like North, East, South, and West. This is the first reason why you must vote wisely.

The second reason is that we are having a rare opportunity to be able to choose our President. In fact, this is the first time in 18 years. So we must take this chance seriously and vote wisely, because our decision will not just affect ourselves, but also our families, not just for this year, next year, but for the next 6 years and even after that.

Do you like what you see in Singapore today? Irrespective whether you like or you don't like, what you see in Singapore today is not because of what is happening in Singapore today? It is because what has happened in the last six years and the six years before that. This is why whoever you choose to be your President will affect you, your families for the next six years and even after that.

So, who should we choose as our next President? In life, there are many types of people. I'll go through four types with you tonight.

First, there is the "yes" man. Have you met a "yes" man? Does "yes" man say no? Actually "yes" man also says no. "Yes" men are those people who will say yes to a certain group of people, no matter how wrong they are. And say no to another group of people, no matter how right they are. Do you want a "yes" man to be your President?

And then there is so called the "pseudo-no" man. What does pseudo mean? Pseudo means not real. For example, if you see someone who appears to be against some policy. But when you look closer, you will see that he is not really against that policy. Then, you know he is a "pseudo-no" man. For these people, they will appear to be against some bad policies. But they will only say no to small things. When it comes to big thing, they will keep quiet. Do you want a "pseudo-no" man to be your President?

And then there is the "real-no" man. These people will say no to everything. Good or bad, they will also say no. Do you want a "no" man to be your President?

Finally, there is a type of person who knows what is right and what is wrong, what is good and what is bad, not for themselves, but for the people of Singapore. For example, for these people, they know minibond is not good for the people of Singapore. So, he will speak up for the people even against big authorities. He will be the voice for the people. This type of person is also independent in their thinking and is not afraid to speak their mind. This type of person will say yes to good policies and no to bad policies. They will not only speak, but will also act. In their action, they will be guided by the values of honesty, fairness, courage, positive attitude, and public service. This type of person is called a "pro-active" man.

Do you want a "pro-active" man to be your President? Do you want a "pro-active" man to be your President? Do you want a "pro-active" man to be your President? Then, vote for Tan Kin Lian!

On 27 August 2011, it was the polling day. The results show that Dr. Tony Tan Keng Yam narrowly won the election with 35.2% of the votes and became the 7th President of Singapore. The other three candidates Dr. Tan Cheng Bock, Mr. Tan Jee Say and Mr. Tan Kin Lian won 34.9%, 25.0% and 4.9% of the votes, respectively.

Even before this presidential election, as my contributions to Singapore and the world, I wrote socio-political articles and they are published in newspapers, magazines or blogs. After the election, I continued to write with renewed vigor. This chapter ends with three selected articles. There are no prizes for guessing what prompted me to write them.

The first is entitled *"Broader perspective on hiring professors"* published by the Straits Times on 12 April, 2014.

All local universities are supported by the Singapore Government, which means they are spending taxpayers" money ("Wanted: Local talent in varsities"; last Saturday). So it is prudent to consider this spending not as an expenditure but as an investment.

In hiring a professor, the university has to pay his salary, as well as fund his research and provide other in-kind support - and these could be done for decades. Hence, the quantum spent on a professor can be large. In return, the professor performs teaching and research as his main duties.

If a university hires a foreign professor, presumably he is "better" in teaching and/or research than his Singaporean counterpart. For the "better" teaching, the return for Singapore is the better education given to local students. For the "better" research, Singapore benefits only if it can make good use of the research findings.

If the foreign professor does not become a Singaporean and commit to Singapore, he takes all that he has received (minus the amount spent here) to another country. He also takes his research expertise with him even though it was built up with Singapore's money.

Hence, for everything that Singapore has invested in the foreign professor, it has to ask whether the returns justify the investment.

In contrast, if the university hires a Singaporean professor, he is likely to remain here for family, social and cultural reasons. As such, the amount he has received and his research expertise stay here.

Even though he may be "poorer" in teaching and research, the return could be higher because the net investment is lower, since all of it stays in Singapore.

When a university uses Singapore's money to hire a professor, isn't it better to use it to support the career of a Singaporean professor rather than a foreigner's?

Indeed, Singapore universities may want to see the hiring of professors from a "broader" perspective, so that the country gets maximum benefit from it.

The second is entitled *"Heaven and hell in Singapore"* published by TR Emeritus on 30 April, 2014.

While Singapore can boast near full employment, it is no secret that there are many Singaporeans, especially PMETs (professionals, managers, engineers, and technicians) who are unemployed or underemployed. There are even more Singaporeans who are working on a suppressed wage because there is no minimum wage in Singapore amidst competition from foreigners. Say for sellers of tissue papers, how much can they make after paying the $120 annual license fee? To live with no or low wage in the most expensive city in the world, Singapore is hell.

At the same time, Singapore can boast 16 entries in the 2014 Forbes list of the world's billionaires. It can also boast of the highest paid political leaders in the world. For them, who can enjoy extravagant cocktail parties at rooftops, Singapore is certainly heaven.

This is indeed the problem in Singapore – co-existence of heaven and hell resulting in a divided society. For those who are in hell, the situation is made worse because they cannot find a way out. To solve or reduce the size of the problem, it is really up to those who are in heaven. They may bridge the gap between heaven and hell by showing understanding, sympathy and offering practical help. If Singapore aspires to become a nation of one united people, it must get these people out, maybe not to heaven but at least out of hell.

The third is entitled *"Can Singapore be one happy family?"* published by TR Emeritus on 30 July 2014.

What are the characteristics of one happy family?

For a family that comprises parents and children, when the children are dependents, the parents will provide all the basic physical needs. They will support their children emotionally and spiritually to the best of their abilities. They will provide learning opportunities for their children so that the children's talents can be developed in the best possible ways.

They will help their children to develop good characters and be their mentors, and set themselves as good examples for their children to follow. They will encourage cooperation rather than competition among the children. They will encourage the more able children to help those who are less able. No matter how weak their children are in their abilities, they will never replace them with children from other families. They will give assurances to their children that they will never be abandoned no matter what. They will share their resources with their children and encourage their children to do likewise. They will encourage their children to be independent thinkers and allow them to fully express themselves. They will give their children freedom to act responsibly without fear of retribution.

For the able children, they will one day become independent and stand on their own within the society. They will be encouraged to live a meaningful life by making a positive contribution to the society, and not be focused on just making economic gains for themselves and the family. They are encouraged to live a life of peace, love, joy and harmony.

When the parents become old and frail, the children will in turn look after their parents' basic physical needs. They will also support their parents emotionally and spiritually to the best of their abilities – till death do them part.

Essentially, the happy family will share their resources and support each other. They will live as one like "we are all one"!

Can Singapore be one happy family? Sure, why not? Apply the above and replace "family" with "country", "parents' with "government" and "children" with "citizens".

May Singapore be one happy family!

How an engineering professor becomes a spiritual philosopher

Chapter 9

Becoming a spiritual philosopher

As mentioned in Chapter 4, I have a deep interest in spirituality. The type of spirituality I practice may be called non-religious spirituality; it is more commonly referred to as new age or new thought spirituality. In order to differentiate this type of spirituality from religion, I refer to religious spirituality as religion, and this type of non-religious spirituality as spirituality. Since some people may not be clear on the differences between these two types of spirituality. In my book *"Wisdom on How to Live Life (Book 4)"*, I have clarified some of the differences. The following is the extract:

> *Harry: Many people don't know the differences between religion and spirituality.*

> Tom: You are right, Guru Harry. So, can you enlighten us?

121

Harry: Sure. First, do you know what causes the confusion?

Tom: No, I am confused.

Harry: Because the terms used in religion are also used in spirituality, and yet they have different meanings.

Tom: So, they are talking about different things?

Harry: So, they are talking about the same things with different meanings.

Tom: That is really confusing.

Harry: Let's see if I can make it clearer.

Tom: As clear as mud?

Harry: Okay, when we talk about religion here, we are mainly referring to organized religion.

Tom: So religious.

Harry: So, religion tends to be practiced in a group and within an organization.

Tom: How about spirituality?

Harry: You can practice it on your own.

Tom: Wow, this is a big difference!

Harry: And since religion is practiced within an organization, the followers tend to follow an organizational truth.

Tom: How about spirituality?

Harry: You are encouraged to follow your own truth.

Tom: But what is the basis of these truths?

Harry: In religion, it is largely based on some doctrine passed down by some earlier masters.

Tom: How about spirituality?

Harry: It is based on your own experience.

Tom: So, what happens when my own experience differs from those stated in the doctrine?

Harry: In religion, you are asked to reject your own experience as truth.

Tom: How about spirituality?

Harry: You are encouraged to accept your own experience as truth.

Tom: Wow, this is another big difference!

Harry: Indeed. This is also why many people are not comfortable with religion.

Tom: Of course, because what they read and hear from religion is not what they experience.

Harry: Right, and this is how spirituality came about.

Tom: How did it come about?

Harry: Spirituality offers a way for people to practice their own truth.

Tom: Their own truth through their own experience.

Harry: This is where they feel comfortable.

Tom: So, people feel comfortable practicing their own truth.

Harry: Since there are many organizations within religion and they may adopt different doctrines, so they tend to be divided.

Tom: How about spirituality?

Harry: Since nobody is forced to follow any particular doctrine, so they cannot be divided.

Tom: Are they united?

Harry: Well, the practice is to encourage everyone to follow his or her own truth, in that sense, they are united.

Tom: So, we are all one.

Harry: Indeed. In religion, it tends to be that we are all one hundred and one.

Tom: Or even one thousand and one.

Harry: This is, of course, the source of religious conflicts.

Tom: How about spirituality?

Harry: As the practice allows everyone to follow his or her own truth, differences are accepted as part of spirituality.

Tom: Like the different colors of our bodies.

Harry: Yet, we are all one.

Tom: Are there other differences between religion and spirituality?

Harry: Religion tends to be very ritualistic.

Tom: Why is it?

Harry: This is a way for the senior followers to assert their "seniority".

Tom: How about spirituality?

Harry: There is little or no ritual.

Tom: Why is it?

Harry: Since everyone is on his or her own path, so there is no such thing as "seniority".

Tom: How about God?

Harry: Religion tends to teach a judgmental, outer God.

Tom: How about spirituality?

Harry: They tend to teach a non-judgmental, inner God.

Tom: God and I are one.

Harry: This is also why religion tends to be fear-based.

Tom: What is fear-based?

Harry: They use fear to motivate people to do good.

Tom: Is it wrong to use fear to motivate people to do good?

Harry: Well, if God is love, and fear is opposite to love, how can fear-based teachings be God's teachings?

Tom: What an enlightened observation!

Harry: But many people are not able to see this.

Tom: Why is this so?

Harry: Because they are misguided?

Tom: So, they instill fear by telling us we are no good.

Harry: Like we are born in sin.

Tom: And we are not good enough to go to Heaven.

Harry: Like we may end up in Hell.

Tom: How about spirituality?

Harry: Since the belief is that we are God, and God is love, spirituality is love-based.

Tom: So, it tends to use love to motivate people to do good.

Harry: That's right. If you are no good, how can you be God?

Tom: But are we good enough to go to Heaven?

Harry: But there is no Heaven.

Tom: Oh yes, that's what you said in the fourth conversation.

Harry: There is another difference in the teaching of God between religion and spirituality.

Tom: What is the difference?

Harry: In religion, you may make contact with God but there are many intermediaries.

Tom: How about spirituality?

Harry: It is the essence of spirituality that you should make direct contact with God without an intermediary.

Tom: Wow, this is another big difference!

Harry: Oh yes, and there is another major difference between religion and spirituality regarding the sources of income.

Tom: What is the major difference?

Harry: With religion, their income usually comes from donations or tithes.

Tom: Is this why religious organizations can give away their products or services for free?

Harry: Sure, because they have already been paid for by donations or tithes.

Tom: How about spirituality?

Harry: They may ask for donation but usually they don't get much.

Tom: So, how do they get their income?

Harry: They usually have to sell their products or services at commercial prices.

Tom: Is this why spiritual products or services are not free?

Harry: If they give away their products or services for free, where is their income coming from?

Tom: Wow, this is a real major difference!

Harry: Okay Tom, are you now clear about the differences between religion and spirituality?

Tom: As clear as a crystal!

In this type of spirituality, the essence is "we are all one". The belief is that at the spiritual level, there is only one soul leading to the saying "There is only one of us". With this belief, the rationale is that if I go to Heaven, then let's all go to Heaven because there is only one of us. If you go to Hell, then let's all go to Hell because there is only one of us. This is why spiritual beings don't curse another to go to Hell. On top of this, spiritual beings don't believe in Heaven and Hell. They believe there is no Heaven and no Hell because they don't favor a reward and punishment system. They prefer not to use fear, like Hell, as the motivator for people to do good. You may then ask why should people do good if there is no reward and punishment or no Heaven and Hell? For spiritual beings, they do good for goodness sake and don't look for rewards, especially spiritual rewards. Isn't this what unconditional love is all about? Okay, while all these are to do with the afterlife, how does the concept "we are all one" work in our physical, everyday life?

The essence is being considerate. Whatever we do, we consider its impacts on another, be it a human, animal or environment. Do unto others as you would have them do unto you. Will the world be better if everyone practices the concept "we are all one"? We will not kill another because if we kill another, it means we kill ourselves. We will not cheat another because if we cheat another, it means we cheat ourselves. So, there will be no war and no financial crisis. On the other hand, if we help another, it means we help ourselves. As the saying goes "Your pain is my pain." So, there will be no hunger and no poverty on Earth. We will naturally live with compassion, integrity and humanness. You see we can be good without living in fear. Wouldn't you call this Heaven on Earth?

For the final part of this chapter, let's take the spiritual concept and see what life is all about.

Is life about making a living or about living a meaningful life? Is life about money and power or is it about soul and spirit? Is life about pleasures of the bodily senses or evolution of the spirit? What is life really about?

If life is about making a living, is it about working to earn money so that we have money to buy food to feed the body? If we believe we are the soul and not the body and the soul lives forever, then do we need to feed the body? If we believe we are the soul, then what is the point of feeding the body and keeping it going? In any case, it doesn't matter how much money we make and how much food we feed the body, the body will still die. So, if making a living is not the purpose of life, then what is?

Is life about being rich and powerful, like Guru Dick? A life with plenty of money and power can be very comfortable, pleasurable and enjoyable. So, can becoming rich and powerful be the purpose of life? Is it meaningful if we wine and dine in a 5-star hotel while our fellow human beings can't afford a meal in a hawker centre? Is it meaningful if we have two cars and oblivious that many of our fellow human beings can't even afford to own one car? Is it meaningful if we earn millions while our fellow human beings are struggling to earn a few dollars? Is it meaningful if we have plenty of power but we use it to suppress our fellow beings so that they live a disempowered life? If life is not about becoming rich and powerful, then why do so many pursue that? What is life about?

On the other hand, if we believe we are the soul and can live forever without any need, then what is life about? If the soul can enjoy peace and love in the spiritual realm, then why does it take up a body and go through the physical struggles of the body? Could it be that the soul uses the physical experience for its spiritual evolution? Could it be that since there is only peace and love in the spiritual realm, there are no challenges there? Could it be that since the soul doesn't have any need and can last forever, there are also no challenges in living? Could it be that for the soul to evolve, it needs to take up the body so as to face all the bodily challenges? The challenges such as how to practice cooperation in the face of competition? How to practice giving in the face of being taking advantage of? How to practice kindness in the face of cruelness? How to practice love in the face of hate? How to practice calmness in the face of turmoil? How to practice peace in the face of conflict? So, by going through all these challenges, could the soul become more evolved? Could life be about becoming a better human being, a better spiritual being and then helping to create a better world?

Amen.

Chapter 10

Epilogue

Since my present physical incarnation has lasted for more than six decades, what have I learned? What is my greatest achievement in this life?

While I am proud of my academic and professional achievements and my loving family, they pale in the shadow of my greatest achievement. Even when I was at the lowest point of my life and faced all the challenges alone, I didn't bow to money and power (I mean I didn't bow to the likes of Guru Dick) and kept my soul intact – this is my greatest achievement. As it happens, this is in line with what I wrote in my book *"Wisdom on How to Live Life (Book 2)"*. The following is the extract:

Tom: Guru Harry, what do you consider as the greatest success in your life?

Harry: I've managed to uphold my principles.

Tom: Throughout your life?

Harry: Throughout my life.

Tom: Did you have to make sacrifices?

Harry: In the normal sense of the word, yes. I may have lost out on money, position and power.

Tom: But you don't consider them as sacrifices?

Harry: No, not at all. You see if you have principles, what are money, position and power?

Tom: But many people give up their principles because of money, position or power.

Harry: Yes, they give up their principles over the tiniest advantage.

Tom: Why do they do that?

Harry: Because they don't know what's really important.

Tom: What is really important?

Harry: Principles.

Tom: Yes, I could have guessed.

Harry: You know there's a saying.

Tom: What is it?

Harry: If you lose your wealth, you lose nothing. If you lose your health, you lose something. If you lose your principles, you lose everything.

In terms of life experiences, I am grateful to the physical, emotional, social, psychological, financial and spiritual challenges. I like to think that because of these challenges, I've grown as a human being and evolved as a human soul. I am grateful to be given the opportunity and responsibilities to look after my mother and mother-in-law for more than one decade. I am grateful for the surreal experience with my mother during her final months in her physical body. I am grateful for the traumatic experience of losing the job at NTU and the subsequent experience of solitude living. I am grateful for the experience of living with an income of a few dollars and finding my way to save ten cents. As a human soul, I am more sympathetic to another human, especially the poor and powerless. I can now see the relevance and importance of politics. I can now better understand the challenges of living spiritually in a non-spiritual society. It is therefore no coincidence that I've been called upon by the Great Spirit to write the books that I have written. To be given the opportunity and responsibilities to author these books, I am eternally grateful.

Last but not least, I like to thank the Great Spirit. While it has been my guiding angel throughout my life, its presence was particularly felt during my latter, trying period. Indeed, in times of triumph, it guided me to humbleness. In times of temptations, it guided me to integrity. In times of crisis, it guided me to stability. In times of despair, it guided me to joy. In times of loneliness, it guided me to peace. In times of disappointments, it guided me to love.

May this sharing be beneficial to you. May peace be with you, always!

Appendix A

List of publications in international academic journals

1. Wong, T.S.W. (1992) *"Discussion of 'Physically Based Flood Features and Frequencies,' by H.W. Shen, G.J. Koch and J.T.B. Obeysekera,"* Journal of Hydraulic Engineering, ASCE, 118(4), 637-638.

2. Chen, C.N. and Wong, T.S.W. (1993) "*Critical Rainfall Duration for Maximum Discharge from Overland Plane,*" Journal of Hydraulic Engineering, ASCE, 119(9), 1040-1045.

3. Wong, T.S.W. and Chen, C.N. (1993) "*Pattern of Flood Peak Increase in Urbanizing Basins with Constant and Variable Slopes,*" Journal of Hydrology, 143(3-4), 339-354.

4. Chen, C.N. and Wong, T.S.W. (1994) *"Closure to 'Critical Rainfall Duration for Maximum Discharge from Overland Plane,'"* Journal of Hydraulic Engineering, ASCE, 120(12), 1484-1486.

5. Wong, T.S.W. (1994) "*Kinematic Wave Method for Determination of Road Drainage Inlet Spacing,*" Advances in Water Resources, 17(6), 329-336.

6. Wong, T.S.W. and Chen, C.N. (1994) "*Use of a Tropical Basin Model to Assess the Importance of Urbanized Land Condition on the Increase of Flood Peak,*" Water Science and Technology, 29(1-2), 155-161.

7. Wong, T.S.W. (1995) "*Discussion of 'Short-Duration-Rainfall Intensity Equations for Drainage Design,' by D.C. Froehlich,*" Journal of Irrigation and Drainage Engineering, ASCE, 121(2), 221.

8. Wong, T.S.W. (1995) "*Time of Concentration Formulae for Planes with Upstream Inflow,*" Hydrological Sciences Journal, 40(5), 663-666.

9. Wong, T.S.W. (1996) "*Influence of Upstream Inflow on Wave Celerity and Time to Equilibrium on an Overland Plane,*" Hydrological Sciences Journal, 41(2), 195-205.

10. Wong, T.S.W. (1996) "*Time of Concentration and Peak Discharge Formulas for Planes in Series,*" Journal of Irrigation and Drainage Engineering, ASCE, 122(4), 256-258.

11. Wong, T.S.W. (1997) "*Discussion of 'Search for Physically Based Runoff Model - a Hydrologic El Dorado?' by D.A. Woolhiser,*" Journal of Hydraulic Engineering, ASCE, 123(9), 830.

12. Wong, T.S.W. and Chen, C.N. (1997) "*Time of Concentration Formula for Sheet Flow of Varying Flow Regime,*" Journal of Hydrologic Engineering, ASCE, 2(3), 136-139.

13. Wong, T.S.W. and Moh, W.H. (1997) "*Effect of Maximum Flood Width on Road Drainage Inlet Spacing,*" Water Science and Technology, 36(8-9), 241-246.

14. Wong, T.S.W. (1998) "*Discussion of 'Rainfall-runoff Processes and Modelling,' by G. O'Loughlin, W. Huber and B. Chocat,*" Journal of Hydraulic Research, IAHR, 36(2), 281-283.

15. Wong, T.S.W. and Li, Y. (1998) "*Assessment of Changes in Overland Time of Concentration for Two Opposing Urbanization Sequences,*" Hydrological Sciences Journal, 43(1), 115-130.

16. Wong, T.S.W. (1999) "*Discussion of 'Balancing Corporate and Personal Values,' by R.H. McCuen,*" Journal of Management in Engineering, ASCE, 15(2), 94.

17. Wong, T.S.W. and Li, Y. (1999) "*Theoretical Assessment of Changes in Design Flood Peak on an Overland Plane for Two Opposing Urbanization Sequences,*" Hydrological Processes, 13(11), 1629-1647.

18. Wong, T.S.W. and Li, Y. (2000) "*Determination of Equilibrium Detention Storage for a Series of Planes,*" Hydrological Sciences Journal, 45(5), 787-790.

19. Wong, T.S.W. (2001) *"Discussion of 'Reverse Routing of Flood Hydrographs using Level Pool Routing,' by C. Zoppou,"* Journal of Hydrologic Engineering, ASCE, 6(3), 264.

20. Wong, T.S.W. (2001) *"Formulas for Time of Travel in Channel with Upstream Inflow,"* Journal of Hydrologic Engineering, ASCE, 6(5), 416-422.

21. Wong, T.S.W. (2002) *"Call for Awakenings in Storm Drainage Design,"* Journal of Hydrologic Engineering, ASCE, 7(1), 1-2.

22. Wong, T.S.W. (2002) *"Discussion of 'Use of Artificial Flood Events to Demonstrate the Invalidity of Simple Mixing Models,' by A. Krein and R. De Sutter,"* Hydrological Sciences Journal, 47(5), 833-837.

23. Wong, T.S.W. (2002) *"Generalized Formula for Time of Travel in Rectangular Channel,"* Journal of Hydrologic Engineering, ASCE, 7(6), 445-448.

24. Wong, T.S.W. (2002) *"Use of Resistance Coefficients Derived from Single Planes to Estimate Time of Concentration of Two-Plane Systems,"* Journal of Hydraulic Research, 40(1), 99-104.

25. Wong, T.S.W. (2003) *"Comparison of Celerity-based with Velocity-based Time-of-concentration of Overland Plane and Time-of-travel in Channel with Upstream Inflow,"* Advances in Water Resources, 26(11), 1171-1175.

26. Wong, T.S.W. (2003) *"Discussion of 'Predicting River Travel Time from Hydraulic Characteristics,' by H.E. Jobson,"* Journal of Hydraulic Engineering, ASCE, 129(5), 412-414.
    (Winner of 2004 J. C. Stevens Award, American Society of Civil Engineers)

27. Wong, T.S.W. and Zhou, M.C. (2003) *"Kinematic Wave Parameters and Time of Travel in Circular Channel Revisited,"* Advances in Water Resources, 26(4), 417-425.

28. Wong, T.S.W. (2004) *"Discussion of 'Extension of TR-55 for Microwatersheds,' by R.H. McCuen and O. Okunola,"* Journal of Hydrologic Engineering, ASCE, 9(1), 68-69.

29. Wong, T.S.W. (2005) *"Assessment of Time of Concentration Formulas for Overland Flow,"* Journal of Irrigation and Drainage Engineering, ASCE, 131(4), 383-387.

30. Wong, T.S.W. (2005) *"Discussion of 'Formula for the Time of Concentration of Runoff,' by Samuel U. Ogbonna,"* Journal of Hydraulic Engineering, ASCE, 131(11), 1024-1025.

31. Wong, T.S.W. (2005) *"Discussion of 'Kinematic Wave Model of Urban Pavement Rainfall-Runoff Subject to Traffic Loadings,' by Chad M. Cristina and John J. Sansalone,"* Journal of Environmental Engineering, ASCE, 131(1), 170.

32. Wong, T.S.W. (2005) *"Influence of Loss Model on Design Discharge of Homogeneous Plane,"* Journal of Irrigation and Drainage Engineering, ASCE, 131(2), 210-217.

33. Wong, T.S.W. (2006) *"Comment on 'A Comparative Fuzzy Logic Approach to Runoff Coefficient and Runoff Estimation' by Z. Sen and A. Altunkaynak,"* Hydrological Processes, 20(18), 3989-3990.

34. Wong, T.S.W. (2006) *"Discussion of 'Editorial – The Peer-review System: Prospects and Challenges,' by Z.W. Kundzewicz and D. Koutsoyiannis,"* Hydrological Sciences Journal, 51(2), 355-356.

35. Wong, T.S.W. (2006) *"Discussion of 'Explicit Solutions of the Manning Equation for Partially Filled Circular Pipes' by O. Akgiray,"* Canadian Journal of Civil Engineering, 32(3), 349-350.

36. Wong, T.S.W. (2006) *"Discussion of 'Uniform and Critical Flow Computations' by R.G. Patil; J.S.R. Murthy; and L.K. Ghosh,"* Journal of Irrigation and Drainage Engineering, ASCE, 132(6), 632.

37. Wong, T.S.W. (2006) *"Physically Based Approach in Hydrology – What is the Benefit?"* Journal of Hydrologic Engineering, ASCE, 11(4), 293-295.

38. Wong, T.S.W. and Lim, C.K. (2006) *"Effect of Loss Model on Evaluation of Manning Roughness Coefficient of Experimental Concrete Catchment,"* Journal of Hydrology, 331(1-2), 205-218.

39. Wong, T.S.W. and Zhou, M.C. (2006) "*Kinematic Wave Parameters for Trapezoidal and Rectangular Channels*," Journal of Hydrologic Engineering, ASCE, 11(2), 173-183.

40. Wong, T.S.W. (2007) "*Discussion of 'Exact Solutions for Normal Depth Problem,' by P. K. Swamee and P. N. Rathie*," Journal of Hydraulic Research, IAHR, 45(4), 567.

41. Chua, L.H.C., Wong, T.S.W. and Sriramula, L.K. (2008) "*Comparison between Kinematic Wave and Artificial Neural Network Models in Event-Based Runoff Simulation for an Overland Plane*," Journal of Hydrology, 357(3-4), 337-348.

42. Wong, T.S.W. (2008) "*Discussion of 'ANN and Fuzzy Logic Models for Simulating Event-Based Rainfall-Runoff' by Gokmen Tayfur and Vijay P. Singh*," Journal of Hydraulic Engineering, ASCE, 134(9), 1400.

43. Wong, T.S.W. (2008) "*Discussion of 'Storm-Water Predictions by Dimensionless Unit Hydrograph' by James C. Y. Guo*," Journal of Irrigation and Drainage Engineering, ASCE, 134(2), 269.

44. Wong, T.S.W. (2008) "*Effect of Channel Shape on Time of Travel and Equilibrium Detention Storage in Channel*," Journal of Hydrologic Engineering, ASCE, 13(3), 189-196.

45. Wong, T.S.W. (2008) "*How Nature uses Overland Flow Regime to Maximize Equilibrium Detention Storage and Flood Attenuation,*" Hydrological Processes, 22(26), 5004-5012.

46. Wong, T.S.W. (2008) "*How to Review or Not to Review a Paper,*" Journal of Professional Issues in Engineering Education and Practice, ASCE, 134(4), 327-328.
   (Ranked 6th of 2008 Top-Ten Article Downloads of Journal of Professional Issues in Engineering Education and Practice)

47. Wong, T.S.W. (2008) "*How to Write an Award-Winning Paper,*" Journal of Professional Issues in Engineering Education and Practice, ASCE, 134(1), 11.
   (Ranked 5th of 2008 Top-Ten Article Downloads of Journal of Professional Issues in Engineering Education and Practice)

48. Wong, T.S.W. (2008) "*Optimum Rainfall Interval and Manning's Roughness Coefficient for Runoff Simulation,*" Journal of Hydrologic Engineering, ASCE, 13(11), 1097-1102.
   (Ranked 2nd of 2008 Top-Ten Article Downloads of Journal of Hydrologic Engineering, and Nominated for 2010 Best Technical Note, Journal of Hydrologic Engineering Awards, American Society of Civil Engineers)

49. Wong, T.S.W. (2009) "*Closure to 'Effect of Channel Shape on Time of Travel and Equilibrium Detention Storage in Channel' by Tommy S. W. Wong,*" Journal of Hydrologic Engineering, ASCE, 14(5), 533.

50. Wong, T.S.W. (2009) "*Evolution of Kinematic Wave Time of Concentration Formulas for Overland Flow,*" Journal of Hydrologic Engineering, ASCE, 14(7), 739-744.

51. Chua, L.H.C. and Wong, T.S.W. (2010) "*Improving Event-Based Rainfall-Runoff Modeling Using a Combined Artificial Neural Network-Kinematic Wave Approach,*" Journal of Hydrology, 390(1-2), 92-107.

52. Talei, A., Chua, L.H.C. and Wong, T.S.W. (2010) "*Evaluation of Rainfall and Discharge Inputs Used by Adaptive Network-Based Fuzzy Inference Systems (ANFIS) in Rainfall-Runoff Modeling,*" Journal of Hydrology, 391(3-4), 248-262.

53. Wong, T.S.W. (2010) "*Discussion of 'Discretization Issues in Travel Time Calculation' by Sandra B. Pavlovic and Glenn E. Moglen,*" Journal of Hydrologic Engineering, ASCE, 15(4), 318-320.

54. Wong, T.S.W. (2010) "*Discussion of 'Volume-Based Imperviousness for Storm Water Designs' by James C. Y. Guo,*" Journal of Irrigation and Drainage Engineering, ASCE, 136(6), 446-449.

55. Chua, L.H.C. and Wong, T.S.W. (2011) *"Runoff Forecasting for an Asphalt Plane by Artificial Neural Networks and Comparisons with Kinematic Wave and Autoregressive Moving Average Models,"* Journal of Hydrology, 397(3-4), 191-201.

56. Chua, L.H.C., Wong, T.S.W. and Wang, X.H. (2011) *"Information Recovery from Measured Data by Linear Artificial Neural Networks - An Example from Rainfall-Runoff Modeling,"* Applied Soft Computing, 11(1), 373-381.

Appendix B

List of public followers of Sathya Sai Baba

- Ravi Shankar musician
- Russian biologist Vladimir Antonov PhD
- Iranian woman journalist Nooshin Mehrabani
- Indian prime ministers Indira Gandhi, Moraji Desai and Manmohar Singh as well as at least 3 prime ministers of Nepal
- a Costa Rican president
- Mexican Luis Muniz
- Italian Catholic priest Mario Mazzoleni
- Icelandic professor of psychology Erlendur Haraldsson
- British animal rights activist Peggy Mason
- Indian nuclear physicist G Venkataraman
- Nigerian priest Charles Ogada
- Japanese classical pianist Masanobu Ikemiya
- **Chinese hydrologist Dr Tommy S W Wong of Singapore**
- Nepal's popular king Birendra Bir Bikram Shah
- Ghana physician George Amoako
- Vema Mukunda who plays the veena in concerts around the world
- Russian yoga teacher Indra Devi

149

- German award winning nature photographer Fred Wunderlich
- Australian Theosophist Howard Murphet, head of the British press section at the Nuremberg trials (which violated international law with premeditated judicial murder)
- Italian Antonio Craxi, brother of the former Italian PM
- Muslim woman poet Zeba Bashiruddin
- Parsi oral surgeon Eruch Fanibunda
- South African Christian Victor Kanu http://wwwsaibabawiences/kanuhtm
- Hollywood screenwriter Arnold Schulman
- Beatle George Harrison
- Nepali film star Shiv Shrestha,
- Marxist editor R K Karanjia of Blitz magazine in Mumbai
- Scifi producer of the Twilight Zone and writer Rod Serling
- Uri Geller, metal bending psychic
- Colonel Roberto Diaz Herrera, whistleblower about sale of drugs in Latin America
- A Russian PM and American president whom I will not mention at this time
- retired tv news anchor Ted Henry
- UK entrepreneur Isaac Tigrett who sold the Hard Rock Cafes upon becoming vegetarian
- Jewish psychiatrist Sam Sandweiss
- Persian poet Begum Tahira Bano Sayeed
- British Dr Keith Critchlow, director of Prince of Wales Institute of Architecture, London
- Cricket legend Sachin Tendulkar

- Art Clokey, syndicated creator of the clay Gumby doll Richard Bock, producer of many films including "The Missing Years of Jesus"
- Sonia Gandhi, daughter in law of Indira Gandhi
- Alice Coltrane pianist
- Maynard Ferguson jazz musician
- Aura measurer Frank Baranowski, PhD, through whose eye prisms 200 reputed masters around the world had auras of 1 to 3 feet Baba's aura, he said, had no limit
- James Peden, author of a book on vegetarian cats and dogs

Appendix C

List of books cited under "Further reading" on "Sathya Sai Baba" page on Wikipedia

1. Howard Murphet (1971) Sai Baba: Man of Miracles pp 208 ISBN 978-0-584-10241-3

2. Samuel H Sandweiss (1975) Sai Baba the Holy Man and the Psychiatrist pp 240 ISBN 978-0-960-09581-0

3. John S Hislop (1985) My Baba and I ISBN 978-0-960-09588-9

4. Phyllis Krystal (1994) Sai Baba: The Ultimate Experience pp 260 ISBN 978-0-877-28794-0

5. Don Mario Mazzoleni (1994) A Catholic Priest Meets Sai Baba pp 285 ISBN 978-0-962-98351-1

6. Erlendur Haraldsson (1997) Modern Miracles: An Investigative Report on These Psychic Phenomena Associated With Sathya Sai Baba pp 315 ISBN 978-0-803-89384-9

7. Vladimir Antonov (2008) Sathya Sai Baba - The Christ Of Our Days pp 38 ISBN 978-1-438-25276-6

8. Tommy S W Wong (2009) How Sai Baba Attracts Without Direct Contact pp 108 ISBN 978-1-448-60416-6

9. Tulasi Srinivas (2010) Winged Faith: Rethinking Globalization and Religious Pluralism Through the Sathya Sai Movement Columbia University Press pp 430 ISBN 978-0-231-14933-4

10. Tommy S W Wong (2011) How Sai Baba Attracts Without Direct Contact (Book 2) pp 102 ISBN 978-1-460-98043-9

Appendix D

List of spiritual books

1. Wong T.S.W. (2009) "*How Sai Baba Attracts Without Direct Contact*," CreateSpace, North Charleston, USA, 108 pp.

2. Wong T.S.W. (2010) "*Wisdom on How to Live Life*," CreateSpace, North Charleston, USA, 152 pp.

3. Wong T.S.W. (2010) "*Wisdom on How to Live Life (Book 2)*," CreateSpace, North Charleston, USA, 110 pp.

4. Wong T.S.W. (2010) "*Wisdom on How to Live Life (Book 3)*," CreateSpace, North Charleston, USA, 124 pp.

5. Wong T.S.W. (2011) "*How Sai Baba Attracts Without Direct Contact (Book 2)*," CreateSpace, North Charleston, USA, 102 pp.

6. Wong T.S.W. (2011) "*Wisdom on How to Live Life (Book 4)*," CreateSpace, North Charleston, USA, 122 pp.

7. Wong T.S.W. (2012) "*Wisdom on How to Live Life (Book 5),*" CreateSpace, North Charleston, USA, 134 pp.

8. Wong T.S.W. (2012) "*Minimum Wage for Low Wage Workers,*" CreateSpace, North Charleston, USA, 42 pp.

9. Wong T.S.W. (2012) "*Wisdom for Spiritual Living,*" CreateSpace, North Charleston, USA, 134 pp.

10. Wong T.S.W. (2013) "*Masters of Life on Meaningful Living,*" CreateSpace, North Charleston, USA, 136 pp.

11. Wong, T.S.W. (2013) "*Wisdom for End-of-Life Living,*" CreateSpace, North Charleston, USA, 62 pp.

12. Wong, T.S.W. (2014) "*Wisdom for Living After Being Fired,*" CreateSpace, North Charleston, USA, 70 pp.

13. Wong, T.S.W. (2014) "*Masters of Life on Good Life and Good Society,*" CreateSpace, North Charleston, USA, 146 pp.

14. Wong, T.S.W. (2015) "*Wisdom for Living as Spiritual Beings,*" CreateSpace, North Charleston, USA, 160 pp.

About the author

As a bestselling author on Amazon, Dr. Tommy Wong is a civil engineer by training, and is a world-renowned hydrologist. Having lived a worldly life, he now lives spiritually in the midst of modern Singapore. Nowadays, he serves the world as a freelance engineering and personal growth consultant. He is also an editor and has authored books of four different genres: engineering, philosophy, self-help and spirituality.

Since 2009, his books have been available on Amazon and many other online bookstores worldwide. In 2012 and 2013, he was featured on the Radio 938LIVE programme "*A Slice of Life Hour*". He has also given talks at the Singapore Writers Festival, Read Fest, Heartlands Book Club, Booktique bookstore, Financial Services Consumer Association, as well as various Meetup groups. Further information about Dr. Wong's work can be found on his website http://wisdomlife.page4.me/ and the FB page https://www.facebook.com/wisdomlivelife.

Made in the USA
Monee, IL
18 September 2022